# Magical Foodlore

## *A Journey through Food from Folklore to Festival*

**WENDY TREVENNOR**

**GREEN MAGIC**

GREEN MAGIC
53 Brooks Road
Street
Somerset
BA16 0PP
England
www.greenmagicpublishing.com

Designed and typeset by Carrigboy, Wells, UK
www.carrigboy.co.uk

ISBN 978 1 915580 36 8

GREEN MAGIC

This book is lovingly dedicated to Alan, my fellow gastronaut in the restaurant of life, and to my wonderful Coven and outer circle for their inspiration and their support and encouragement in all aspects of my life, as well as my publisher Pete, who is always so encouraging.

# Acknowledgements

My thanks to my good friend Karen Thomas, a proofreader par excellence who does not just exercise care and patience in proofreading and checking my work but also suggests ideas of her own.

To Karen, and to Diane Maxey and Mandy Senior for their help with recipes.

# Contents

# Introduction

"Food is our common ground, a universal experience."

– James Andrew Beard.

The importance of food to humans transcends mere sustenance or the satisfying of appetite. We don't simply eat to survive; we celebrate existence, we affirm life. A shared meal can bind families, forge friendships, and mark the rites of passage of lives – from births and weddings to festivals and farewells. We eat for life and joy, for love, for celebration, for fellowship, for magic.

Food carries identity. A single recipe can tell the story of a homeland, an era, or a community's beliefs. It distinguishes one region from another, serves as a silent emblem of class or faith, and becomes a language through which we claim belonging. When strangers break bread together, they enter a universal ritual of hospitality and trust.

Beyond earthly needs, food enters the sacred. In rituals and ceremonies, we offer bread, wine, fruits, herbs, or spices to honour deities, invoke protection, or heal the spirit. These ancient practices reveal an unexpected magic: food as conduit between the mundane and the divine, nourishing body, heart, and soul in equal measure.

This book explores the world of food from a spiritual and magical perspective, from the stories we all grew up with ("Who's been eating *my* porridge?") to the use of food in ritual, spellworking and the worship of the Gods. Not just a witchy recipe book (although there are recipes too!),

*Magical Foodlore* will tell you about uses for food you never suspected, as well as the historical precedents, the folk stories and folk songs, and the superstitions which may be more ancient than we know. It will explain the sacredness of the kitchen, as the heart of the home and the heart also of comfort, sustenance and enjoyment, of caring for the family, welcoming guests and exercising those domestic magics which every housewife, parent, cook or single person works – whether they are a domestic goddess at the heart of a large family or a working person living alone who knows and honours the pleasures of the table – whether or not they are aware of the potential of food as a magical tool.

Taking the importance of food a little further, we will then examine its use in ways that go beyond nourishing the body, that go some way towards feeding the soul and exploring our magical potential. For food, like almost any physical sphere, has potential far beyond what is initially perceived. And why should this surprise us? Too long has the Christian idea that spirit and body are totally separate entities restricted our thinking and our imagination. As we are all part of the Gods, so too is what we eat, and it has the same potential for growth and power as any other item we might use for our spiritual and magical development.

CHAPTER ONE

# How Meat Made Man ... and How Food Broke Us

"Tell me what you eat, and I will tell you what you are."

– Jean Brillat-Savarin.

Imagine the life of our distant ancestors. While for us food is a punctual and pleasant diversion from the day's chores and cares, for them it was a permanent preoccupation, for their life gave them no assurances as to where their next meal was coming from, or whether it would arrive at all. Not for them the astonishing and colourful variety of selected and packaged foods, fresh, dried, frozen, preserved, chilled, bottled, tinned or vacuum-packed, displayed in the supermarket and even delivered to the door. Not for them the enticing frontages of restaurants and cafés, or the travelling pizza summoned by telephone call or email, or the succulent sandwich available, with other snacks, sweets and drinks, even at non-food outlets such as petrol stations, airports and railway stations.

Life was, as Thomas Hobbes remarked, "nasty, brutish and short" for our forebears ... and indeed continues to be for too many people of poorer and war-torn nations in the world today, and food is still a problem for these unfortunates, as it was for early Man millions of years ago.

This is not an archaeological book, so I will do no more than touch upon the transformation that food created – and continues to create – in humankind: the fact that food, far from being just fuel for our active bodies, could actually be said to have created us as a species. Make no mistake: meat made us. We know that other closely related apes, especially chimpanzees but also bonobos and baboons, will eat meat if they can, scavenging the remains of predators' kills or even cannibalising weaker members of their own species. Yet they mainly live on leaves, fruit, nuts and seeds, roots and tubers and maybe also insects and grubs. Proto-humans certainly began to eat meat at an early stage ... and what a transformation this produced! The *Expensive Tissue Hypothesis* of Aiello and Wheeler puts forward the theory that early humans began to eat carrion to supplement their largely vegetarian diet, thus acquiring the nutritional wherewithal to begin developing a much larger brain – though this was at the expense of other organs, particularly the gut. It became a sort of vicious circle: we ate meat and had big brains, so we couldn't support a bigger gut to digest plant food or have it as our main source of nourishment, so we had to eat meat ... Our brains actually consume between a fifth and a quarter of our resting daily calorie expenditure, or between 300 and 500 calories, so they truly are 'expensive tissue'. Plant eaters generally need much more *apparatus* to draw enough nutrition from their protein- and calorie-poor diet; cows, sheep and other ruminants have multiple stomachs and chew regurgitated cud; lagomorphs produce two kinds of droppings, eating the first kind to re-digest them; and koalas, who can lay claim to having the poorest diet on the planet, nutrient-poor and filled with toxins, use a very long gut and bacterial fermentation to break down their eucalyptus leaf meals. These are all procedures necessary to break down the cell walls, or cellulose, of the grass and other plant cells, into useful sugars.

Meat eating started our forebears on the path that led to their becoming Homo sapiens, the dominant species on the planet. Their new meat-eating habits – and the larger brains that began to develop as a result of this protein-rich diet – led them to start developing tools, starting with very simple objects like heavy stones for smashing open marrowbones and flint blades for cutting through tissue. Later they would develop weapons, whether for ambushing predators and taking their kills by force or for hunting their own prey. At some stage, they also learned to cook their meat with fire, thus rendering it not only easier to digest but a lot less hazardous in terms of bacteria and parasites and certainly more enjoyable to eat.

Fast forward some two and a half million years, and the now more advanced humans are ploughing the fields and scattering, growing a variety of pulses for food and flax for clothing. Animals were herded, and fowls such as ducks, geese and chickens were kept. Agriculture meant more leisure for early peoples, who did not have to be on the move constantly and thus had the freedom to start developing religion, art and culture. And of course, they also grew cereals like wheat, barley, oats, emmer, maize, rice and rye, for bread of a primitive kind was already part of the human diet and would soon grow to have overwhelming importance to us. These early breads, hardly meriting the name, were little more than smashed grass seeds mixed with water and seared over a fire, but by 6000 BCE yeasts had entered the equation, and bread that we would recognise as such today had started to be made. If meat made us what we are, bread has kept us going as a species and opened our horizons. Common to all peoples, all countries and all cultures, it is quite simply the universal staple, and in human imagination, spirituality, anecdote and story carries more meaning than its simple composition would seem to justify.

For bread reversed the equation that farming meant staying in one place, as opposed to the nomadic lifestyle of the hunter-gatherers. Bread could be carried. Bread did not go rotten and could therefore fuel a new type of traveller. Bread turned us into travellers again, and the discovery of ways to seek out and preserve other foods, salting and drying meat and fish, turned us into explorers, conquerors.

And explorers we have remained for the rest of our history, from primitive humans perhaps driven from an area by drought or disease, through Vikings plundering farms and Tudor adventurers ransacking the New World for tomatoes and potatoes, to modern gastro-tourists in search of delicious food from other cultures; we are driven onwards by curiosity, hunger and appetite.

Food is a multifaceted blessing: what we learn at our mothers' and grandmothers' tables constitutes what we understand as basic food, food that can be trusted, food that brings happy memories. As the Chinese writer and philosopher Lin Yutang memorably said, "Patriotism is the love of the food one ate as a child."

But God, it was dull! English food was once notorious for being boring, and it was, up until the later 20th century, especially for the poor. Most urban working-class English children of my generation (Baby Boomers) subsisted on a diet of Sunday roast, which became cold meat on Monday and stretched to shepherd's pie on Tuesday, followed by sausages and rissoles … some families adhered, for half-forgotten religious reasons, to fish on Fridays. And so it went on, week after week with little or no variation, all served up with the obligatory potatoes and two veg (usually carrots and peas). Desserts were farinaceous concoctions, baked or boiled and always served with custard. Bread and butter, beans on toast and a vile gelatinous pink tinned ham, the name of which has gone down in history as something unwanted, formed an appreciable part of the diet. Many things were tinned … I remember even potato salad and dairy cream being bought tinned instead of fresh because they were cheaper that way and, in an era in which not all households had a fridge, could be relied on to stay fresh (or at least untainted). Work canteens and school meals followed the same pattern. Yes, we had flavourings. We had salt and white pepper (people did not usually buy black pepper in those times); we had herbs, and we had more special flavours: cloves, ginger, nutmeg, allspice, and cinnamon for Christmas and other special baking. These had been with us for centuries, originally imported from the East and used to disguise the flavour of meat that had gone past its sell-by date. But they were very few and sparingly used.

But within our lifetimes, or those of our parents, this was set to change gloriously. One of the great blessings of the 20th century was the influx of people of other races from within what had been the British Empire: firstly and famously, the Indian restaurant, with its flock wallpaper and piped sitar music, became a common fixture in every high street … Our eyes (and our mouths) were opened to extraordinary new flavours. It was an epiphany for a people that had once disdained French food – because it had garlic and sauces. Many people's anxieties about oil and garlic and chillis and other foreign spices were laid to rest once they had experienced this exquisite new cuisine with all its exotic richness (hearing the Indian waiter speak in a broad Cockney accent to his colleague in an unguarded moment probably helped reassure them as well!). Strange and exotic vegetables and fruits began to appear in the shops: peppers, fresh chillis, garlic, aubergines, pak choi, mangoes, lychees, squashes, avocadoes ... as with tomatoes two or three generations earlier, ordinary British people did not really know what to do with these, but they soon found out. Now, with a huge variety available in the supermarket and Chinese, French, Italian, Japanese, Korean, Caribbean, Spanish and many other cuisines from everywhere on the planet represented in larger cities and our TV screens alight with chefs of every nationality, this can truly be said to be a Golden Age of food.

Many people have said that food is the universal language, and I believe that this delicious invasion did us a great deal of good, not just in the UK but in all nations where racial prejudice reared its sorry head. We loved their food, so gradually came to accept them as fellow human beings with a slightly different outlook and culture...but with expertise in producing extraordinary food that made them welcome.

One of the biggest changes the 20th century wrought in British people's lives was that everyday food (as opposed to special meals at festivals and celebrations) moved on from being necessary and utilitarian to becoming a pastime, a leisure activity (and in some cases, an addiction). One of my favourite authors, Flora Thompson, describes in *Lark Rise to Candleford* how the mothers of the late 19th-century rural poor fed their families: *"The square of bacon was cut, the roly-poly made and the black cooking pot was slung over the fire at four o'clock; for wages still stood at ten shillings* (50p) *a week, and they knew that their mothers' way was the only way to nourish their husbands and children on so small a sum."* Poverty clearly played the largest role in the dullness and repetitiveness of these scanty meals: this was food eaten, not without enjoyment, I am sure, but as nourishment, as fuel, and for no other reason.

Move on less than a century from *Lark Rise*, and already food is being presented to ordinary people as something other than nutrition. For with the influx of more interesting ingredients from other countries came the rise of the TV chef, the food fashionista, the influencer. From 1946, when the first British TV chef Philip Harben demonstrated lobster vol-au-vents to an audience who had previously only been able to hear him on the radio, food started to become more than food. It became a leisure activity, a hobby and a cause of pride and status. The internet has got in on the act as well, and many a pleasant hour can be spent watching TikTok and YouTube videos on cookery … perhaps while ordering takeaway food online!

The wealthy have always gloried in their ability to eat well and feed their guests rich, extraordinary and fashionable food, but now this ceased to be their exclusive preserve. Ordinary people with lower incomes and poorer education could not only be inspired by these new media but also had access to the means to fulfil their aspirations.

Status continues to be an ingredient. If satisfying hunger were the only reason for eating, we would settle for street food or fast food (outlets for which spread across the world from the 1940s), or eat at home. Paying hundreds of pounds for an over-presented and unsatisfying meal at a high-status restaurant is the preserve of the wealthy, or those wishing to appear as such to impress a date or work contact – less about the food than the impression one wishes to make. After all, the best and tastiest food is often that which originated in poverty: pasta and pizza, the Irish stew, the Cornish pasty, the Yorkshire pudding, polenta and cornbread, sausages of all kinds, and meatloaf, the soul foods still loved today by people of African American descent, and even just plain ol' toast.

At the same time, interest in nutrition itself, as the science of nourishing the body in as complete and healthy a way as possible, has risen to a multimillion-pound industry. Whole sections of supermarket aisles are packed with vitamin tablets, oil capsules, herbal supplements, spice capsules, alternative remedies for colds, hay fever, insomnia, menopause symptoms, hair loss, constipation, indigestion, and erectile dysfunction. Food as medicine, a concept dating back all the way to the Ancient Egyptians and the Ancient Chinese and now a re-emerging trend in the medical community, has increasing relevance in an age where too many families live on fast food and junk food, an age where fewer and fewer children and young people are taught to cook in schools or at home, and most of all an age where the fast pace of life precludes many of the kitchen practices that kept our grandparents nourished on a small income and on cheaper ingredients.

Meat made us, but did food also break us? In the next section, we will look at the negative side of modern food habits and how they have impacted our cultures and our bodies.

Abundance sounds like an entirely positive state, and yet like so many apparently good things, it has its shadow side. With the increasing wealth and better nutrition of the developed countries of the West, another 20th- and 21st-century phenomenon connected with food began to rear its ugly head. Just as food made mankind, it seems it can also break us, and with advances in science as time has gone on, modern technology has combined with human fears and weaknesses to turn food into a health and well-being catastrophe.

As life gets easier, people seem to become more and more vulnerable, in an apparent reaction to the difficulties of the past. Where once we were obliged to work hard for every piece of bread, now we are overwhelmed with food: it is advertised constantly on all media wherever we go, totally available, easy to prepare or ready-made, and loaded with excess calories, pumped full of fats and sugars. No wonder that we are all a lot fatter than we used to be. And overconsumption and obesity are no longer the preserve of the rich; the relative cheapness of food has combined with general inactivity and couch-potato lifestyles to associate overweight and obesity more closely with the lower classes of society. In the West this has reached a nightmare situation, with 64% of the UK population being overweight and 29% of these being clinically obese; in the US this rises to 70%, with 42% of those being considered obese. Obesity is understood as having a BMI (body mass index, or weight to height ratio) of 30 or more, with morbid obesity defined as having a BMI of 50 or more. This has fuelled an epidemic of related conditions, especially heart disease and type 2 diabetes. Up to 4.5 million people – that is around 15% of the total population – are estimated to have type 2 diabetes in the UK, and in the US it is 35 million – almost 10%. Type 2 diabetes, which is more likely in older people but overwhelmingly more likely in overweight and obese people, develops when the body's systems begin to cease responding to the hormone insulin (possibly due at least in part to the wild swings of blood sugar levels and overproduction of insulin which go with a lifestyle of overeating rich and sugary foods), and the condition basically trashes the body's organs, especially the heart, nerves, kidneys, and eyes.

Piling pity on horror, this grim journey has culminated in the phenomenon of the super-obese and the gruesome voyeurism of TV 'fat porn' programmes like *My 600lb Life.*

Is it what we eat? Should we be turning away from fatty, sugary foods? A look at past times would seem to suggest that this is not the answer. Children in my generation were fed dripping (basically lard with attitude) on toast. My husband, as a child, was given sugar sandwiches. Sugar was added to babies' feeds or given to them on dummies dipped in the sugar bowl. White bread held sway. Meat and farmed animals generally were a lot less lean than they are today. We had biscuits and cake and jam and pudding every day, butter on everything, and everyone took sugar in their tea, usually two spoons full. Kids' sweets were never rationed by parents, except just before meals, and never because they were unhealthy, except for the teeth. Yet the rate of obesity was minimal: I remember there being no more than a couple of plump kids in my class at school.

"If only chips were low-calorie and lettuce were fattening!" is the eternal cry of the poor dieter restricted to a constant round of rabbit food, but we seem to be hardwired to prefer high-calorie, high-fat and sugary foods, a preference dictated by the DNA of our ancient forebears, who perforce scraped the environment for every mouthful and needed to optimise nutritional intake in exactly the opposite way to what we now try to do. Life is in some ways harder for the food addict than for the alcoholic: a recovering alcoholic can avoid pubs and bars, not buy wine or spirits, and enlist their friends in supporting them to stick to soft drinks in an unavoidably alcohol-laden situation. But no one can escape the presence or the need for food. As the desperation of serial dieters grows, many resort to alternative diets and remedies – usually sponsored by celebrities: the paleo diet, the keto or Atkins diet, the cabbage soup diet, the grapefruit diet, Himalayan pink salt, and intermittent fasting (if I sound unsympathetic, believe me I am not: I have been there myself). The last desperate attempt may involve bariatric surgery, if it is permitted by the doctor and can be afforded, or the new array of weight loss injections such as Mounjaro and Wegovy. These last two options certainly work in the short term, but they do not solve the underlying problem of overeating and poor lifestyle choices.

As a friend jested on Facebook the other day, Lewis Carroll's Alice found magical cakes in Wonderland with 'Eat me' written on them in currants … if he could only find the ones that make you grow smaller!

Maybe it is not what we eat but how much. And maybe it is more to do with how physically active we are. The bottom line, as any dietician will tell you, is balancing the equation of calories in and calories out: eat less than you need and you will get thinner. Eat too many, and the build-up of fat is the result. In an age when few people walk or cycle, when it is normal to take your children to school in the car even when it is only a couple of streets away, when you do not need to leave the sofa even to change channels, we are not burning enough calories for the amount of food we eat. Housework is accomplished at the flick of a switch, whether it is cleaning, laundry or chopping and preparing food. Heating fuel comes in a pipe or a tanker lorry, so no one has to labour outside splitting logs or carrying coal. Very few people work as our great grandparents did, and in the workplace it is the same. Few workers carry heavy loads or push trucks or turn heavy machinery manually.

In earlier times, being fat was considered quite desirable: in an era when many scraped by on not quite enough food, being overweight marked you out as being a much more successful person, someone who could afford to gorge on rich foods and not do too much physical work either. Women with more generous curves were admired, as they looked like the women of successful men. I have heard it said that Marilyn Monroe was the last actress permitted to have a tummy. But the era saw greater general affluence, and fashion – which always seems to buck the trend in terms of what real people are looking like – suddenly changed its course and began to focus on skinny and ever-skinnier models. In the mid-1960s, the six-and-a-half stone (47kg) Twiggy was suddenly the paradigm of feminine beauty.

Suddenly slimness became the most desirable feminine physical trait, and this seemed to set off a series of problems with human diet and human health. 'Anorexia nervosa' was not a term any layperson had heard before, but since the 1960s it has gradually become a serious health problem, with numbers rising around 36% every five years and at least eight million people in the UK currently suffering from this potentially fatal condition, especially (but not exclusively) young women aged 13 to 24. It is hardly surprising. Young persons are faced with images of slender, semi-clad or nude women wherever they go, on online media, TV, billboards, and in magazines. Until just ten years ago, the infamous 'Page Three' models in *the Sun*, supposedly a family newspaper, were displayed topless or totally nude for any child to pick up and see. What message would an impressionable young girl take from all of this?

With the growth of online media and the development of sciences like AI, which can distort and change true images so they appear quite different, it has become still more serious, with adolescent and pre-adolescent children (usually girls) becoming the target of online bullying, which frequently leads to poor body image and consequent anorexia, bulimia or binge-eating disorders. 'Fat' is a word now used generally as an insult by the young, often regardless of the body shape of the victim. Adding images of models into the mix, computer enhanced to have unnaturally slim bodies and unrealistically beautiful features, can only fuel the insecurities that lead to eating disorders in young, vulnerable people. In the most severe cases young (and not-so-young) people have actually starved themselves to death or into a state of health which threatens and shortens their lives. We all remember the beautiful, talented, but tragic Karen Carpenter.

CHAPTER TWO

# Food Glorious Food

"There is no sincerer love than the love of food."

– George Bernard Shaw.

As we have seen in the previous chapter, our relationship with food is complex, a love-hate relationship which makes primal scene look as innocent and wholesome as the morning dew on the grass. But for the most part, we celebrate our hunger and our eating. We love food, so we call people we love by food-related names (honey, pumpkin, chicken, sweetcake, sugar, cupcake, muffin, sweetie pie), and people who attract us sexually 'crumpet', 'a dish', 'beefcake' or 'cheesecake'. The sexual parts of the body also have historically had a range of food-based slang terms, with which I am sure most of you are familiar. There is even a range of fetishes called 'sitophilia' involving the use of food in sexual practices. We name flowers and colours and other things that inspire us after foodstuffs. While foods can be named after people who invented or inspired them (the sandwich after the 4th Earl of Sandwich, the Margherita pizza after Queen Margherita of Savoy, the Peach Melba after the soprano Dame Nellie Melba, the meringue dessert Pavlova after the Russian ballerina Anna Pavlova, and Beef Wellington after Arthur Wellesley, 1st Duke of Wellington), people can also be named after foods (Candy, Basil, Cherry, Chardonnay, Peaches, Clementine). Above all, we use food to celebrate, to reward, and to treat those we love.

Whether it is a box of chocolates for your girlfriend or a posh dinner out for your son who has just graduated, we love to treat our loved ones. It's a universal language of love and kindness. And after all … like the quality of mercy, the act of giving benefits the giver as well as the receiver, so we get some too! From our Palaeolithic ancestors who gave food to old or ailing members of the tribe and titbits to wives, concubines or children who had pleased them, the food treat is something common to all peoples and all ages. Community eating is as old as humanity and has gained great significance over the ages. 21st-century families may make a point of sitting down and eating dinner together – if only on trays before the TV – because they may not otherwise see one another a great deal during the working week. Families who are reuniting for some occasion always plan a special meal; indeed, such occasions are usually planned *around* the meal or meals.

But even when generosity or a desire to help or treat someone is not involved, we treat ourselves whenever we cook. Food and its preparation are life-affirming, even therapeutic.

The immortal Delia Smith said: "If you sometimes feel depressed or let down, if you're suffering from the pressures of life, or simply having a plain old grey day, my advice is to roast a chicken. I'm not precisely sure why, but there is, and always has been, some magical 'cure-all' involved in the whole process. Sometimes you need to turn your back on the complications of life, give yourself some space and become homespun and happy for just a couple of hours." A dish that is pleasant to prepare, fills the whole house with savoury aromas and promises a delicious treat when it is ready … win-win! Delia also said much the same about the process of baking a cake, and another TV cook, Mary Berry, described cooking as "mental and physical therapy", in my opinion quite correctly.

To demonstrate further the euphoric effect that these delicious aromas have on us, those of baking bread or cake and freshly brewed coffee are also used, rather more cynically, by house sellers and bakeries when they brew coffee and bake bread together to entice the buyer!

Cooking fills you with pleasure and comfort, relieves stress by taking your mind off your worries and filling you instead with pleasurable anticipation and positive mindfulness, encourages creativity and promotes healthy eating (no one puts preservatives or MSG into their own homemade food). You might be looking forward to eating the food yourself, or you may be making something that can be given away, like jam and preserves or cookies; the result is the same: a calm and positive mood and a sense of achievement. My husband laughs at what he calls my "cosy warm kitchen days", when I lock myself away in the kitchen for batch cooking or preparation of special treats, but they do me the world of good.

Food varies enormously across the world, depending on soil, native fauna and flora, climate and tradition. Like Scots tartan, which was supposedly created from the dye plants indigenous to the valley where the clan bearing it lived, it is deeply regional ... yet there is also creep. From Asian fusion to the declaration of the tikka masala curry in 2001 as "the true British national dish", food, like language, is subject to influences – as US TV chef JJ Johnson memorably said, "Migration impacts the way we cook," and he described cooking and food as "the universal language." Don't forget: the Italians did not invent pasta ... it came from China, and we British did not have our favourite vegetable, the potato, as a major crop until the middle of the 18th century or one of our favourite desserts, rice pudding, until the British Raj. Our Christmas lunch favourite, the turkey, came from North America as a luxury item and did not gain popularity with ordinary people until the mid-20th century. US favourite dishes – the hamburger, apple pie, pizza and chilli – have almost all arrived there from other cultures. The tomato, now known, grown, appreciated and used worldwide and a vital constituent of almost all savoury Italian food, originally came from South America, although, as a member of the often toxic nightshade family, it was greeted with initial suspicion. The 16th-century *Columbian Exchange*, when explorers brought back all sorts of strange fruits and vegetables from the newly discovered Americas, transformed many national cuisines: imagine Italy without tomatoes or polenta, India without chillis, or Spain without paprika. And remember: the discovery of the Americas themselves happened because the explorer Christopher Columbus was trying to find an alternative route to the East, where spices were traded.

Just as food varies, festivals and celebrations vary, and every culture has its own set of dishes traditionally prepared for these occasions from local ingredients and using local culinary methods. These special foods and dishes for festivals, particularly for spiritual ones, have become permanently (and often exclusively) associated with that festival (who eats mince pies, except at Christmas?). Often the food is associated with the festival because of its availability at that time of the year: pumpkin soup and pumpkin pie for Halloween, for example, and fresh eggs and a leg of spring lamb at Easter.

Sometimes these foods have a symbolic meaning within the faith that produced them, like unleavened bread at Passover in Judaism, which recalls the hasty preparation of provisions for the flight from Egypt, while on the Shabat they eat *cholent*, a slow-cooked stew which can be prepared the previous day, to honour the idea of God resting on the seventh day after creating the world. Hot cross buns are served in Christian countries on Good Friday to represent the crucifixion of Christ, though these are often available all year round in many countries, including the UK. They had their origins in pre-Christian traditions, with cakes being marked with a cross to represent the four seasons or moon phases, while the Saxons marked them to honour the Goddess Eostre. In folklore, a recommended use for these delicious buns was to hang them in the kitchen to protect the home from evil spirits!

Other foods are less specific in their meaning but still tied to the festival: chocolate Easter eggs, hens' eggs and roast lamb to symbolise new life at Easter in Christianity; sweetened rice pudding at Vesak (Buddha Jayanti, Buddha's birthday); and jiaozi dumplings at the Chinese New Year for prosperity. Stollen, a rich marzipan-based bread confection produced in Germany for Christmas, is made with large amounts of butter, which was not supposed to be eaten during Advent (the run-up to Christmas). But Pope Innocent VIII sanctioned this use of butter in the 15th century – provided the bakers donated towards the building of the Freiberg Minster and other churches, which perhaps gave it an odour (or even a flavour) of sanctity.

Cake has always held a special place at celebrations, whether it is the snowy multi-tiered perfection of a wedding cake or the alcohol- and spice-filled richness of Christmas cake or Scandinavian *kransekage* or Chinese Mid-Autumn Festival mooncakes. The cake has often been the centrepiece of the feast because it is made in advance and can be decorated to a colourful splendour. Cake probably became a special event in the first place because its ingredients, especially sugar and spices, were once expensive and hard to obtain, so it was kept for very special occasions. Large cakes served at rich banquets began to be decorated with what we would now recognise as icing from the 17th century, and cake art has continued to grow in popularity, with icing art (sugarcraft) now a popular hobby, with classes, websites and magazines devoted to it, and special celebration cakes being produced with amazing 3D art and even edible photographic images applied as toppings.

Meats were the other luxury that even the poor would strive to put on the table at festivals: in Europe, the Christmas meal would usually be beef or a goose, with the turkey not becoming common until the 20th century. Sometimes the festivals and their associated feasting served simply to point up the often astonishing difference between the classes: while the rich enjoyed such whimsies as the 'cockentrice', half a small pig sewn to the neckless body of a fowl and served as an edible chimaera, the poor of previous centuries might make do with home-cured bacon, sausages, blood puddings or offal, while at other times meat of any kind played an insignificant role in their diets.

And we must not forget the drinks that accompany these feasts. Historically, British people drank a great deal of beer: its method of preparation saved many a person from the typhoid and cholera that lurked in the water supply, but wine was not generally made here, as in most of Britain grapes do not do well – or did not, before climate change

– outside glasshouses. Wine itself has, to British ears, a romantic, celebratory, *special occasion* sound, whereas the French often drink *vin ordinaire* at every meal. And wine also has its place at festivals and celebrations. But it is champagne that instantly conjures a vision of glasses being clinked in a toast, paper streamers, wedding bells, glitter, silver service, best clothes and finery, and joyful smiles. There is something about the sparkle produced by the second fermentation of the *methode champenoise* that ties it irrevocably to parties and other glitzy events where no expense has been spared – as its price reflects!

The reverse side of the celebration food coin is the abstention from certain foods at certain times, or altogether, in many traditions. The best known of these are the *kosher* and *haram/halal* traditions of Jews and Muslims, in which meat is prepared in a certain way and some foods, notably pork, are never eaten. Jews have an extensive list of forbidden foods which includes dishes that use meat and dairy products together, shellfish, meat from any animal that does not have cloven hooves, fish that do not have scales and carnivorous birds. Muslims are also forbidden to drink alcohol. Many Hindus and Buddhists are vegetarians, and those who do eat meat abstain from beef, as the cow is sacred to their faith: fortunately, they are free to eat dairy foods, which are plentiful in India because of the protected status of cows. The Chinese, on the other hand, have historically avoided cow's milk and milk products, as they are genetically predisposed to being lactose-intolerant and milk (other than soy milk) has never been a significant part of their diet.

But banned and taboo foods are part of an ancient and almost universal tradition of dietary laws which goes back many thousands of years and is usually linked to religion, though it may have had its origins in ancient poisonings and illnesses brought about by eating unsuitable foods, perhaps in a hot climate (even today we say, 'Only eat oysters in a month with an 'r' in it', as from May to August the hot weather could cause the fish to spoil quickly and develop toxins). In Ancient Egypt, the Nile Oxyrhynchus, a species of elephantfish, was taboo, as it was believed to have eaten the severed penis of Osiris after his brother Set murdered him and cut his body into pieces. In Ancient Greece, localised taboos included the eating of horsemeat and bear meat, while in Ancient Rome a slightly different focus on taboo was presented in the *sumptuary laws*, which were aimed at preventing extravagance by the richer classes in both food, lifestyle and dress to prevent waste and decadence and to stop the middle classes from trying to copy or compete with the patrician class. These laws banned the serving of rich, rare and fattened foods, including dormice, dolphins, shellfish, force-fattened and imported birds, and undiluted wine (serving wine neat was considered ill-bred).

In Christianity, food restrictions – rather than taboos – have included fasting and a deliberately poor diet at some times of the year, including the six weeks of Lent, to honour the tradition of Christ fasting and praying for 40 days in the wilderness before beginning his work of preaching and healing. Lent traditions include a poor diet with little or no meat, butter, eggs or milk (and Shrove 'pancake' Tuesday is provided beforehand to use up these ingredients!), and some people may give up other pleasures, perhaps tea and coffee, smoking or TV, and include extra prayer and meditation or Bible-reading. Strict Catholics still keep to the practice of eating only fish on Fridays, rather than meat, as a way of honouring Christ and recalling his crucifixion on this day of the week. The custom of fasting is also traditional in other religions, such as the dawn to dusk fast at the New Year, or Ramadan in Islam, which forbids any food and any drink – even water – or other indulgences such as sex and smoking. Other faiths may have voluntary fasting customs, including Judaism, Hinduism, Jainism and Buddhism.

Other forms of taboo are not dictated by religious authority but arise out of custom and disgust: few people in Britain would relish eating a fried tarantula, which is, however, a delicacy in Cambodia, or ants, which are eaten coated in chocolate in Mexico and some African countries. In the West, people are generally averse to the idea of eating insects, although some insect material has started to be included in some foods now available, including crickets milled into bread flour (available online). Yet in Asian, African and South American countries, they may form a significant part of the diet, and this idea is starting to creep into Europe as well. Perhaps reading about "delicious locusts" in the Bible has to some extent prepared our minds for this concept.

The British are notorious for their conservatism in the matter of food, and many quite acceptable meats which are eaten across Europe are greeted by many UK people with a grimace of disgust: horsemeat, goat, frogs' legs, snails and many forms of offal which are not now (if they ever were) available in the UK, such as brains, testicles and udders. But to gustatory disgust is added sheer horror at the idea of eating dogs and cats, a custom which still pertains in many Asian countries, notably South Korea, where dogs are actually farmed for their meat – although I am pleased to report that dog meat is now to be banned in South Korea by

February 2027 as attitudes and sensitivities change. Some animal welfare charities there have been helping farmers for some time to transition to other ways of earning a living (for example, mushroom farming) and the dogs are taken for rehoming. But it remains prevalent in North Korea. The practice is also, oddly, known in Switzerland, where people are legally permitted to eat dog or cat meat as long as it is not purchased, meaning they can only eat their own pets!

A further consideration is that of ethical eating: vegetarianism and veganism are not confined to paganism but are widespread in many faiths, but there are other moral considerations, such as air miles, packaging and shelf life, and the destruction of natural areas for farming (e.g., palm oil). Some people vote with their feet to express disapproval for a regime – for example, refusing to buy oranges from South Africa during apartheid and currently the boycotting of Israeli products in the wake of the Israel-Gaza war.

Finally, the strongest taboo of all, yet the least talked about, is that against eating human flesh: cannibalism. Sit down, Hannibal! The idea fills most normal people with utter abhorrence, yet it is an ancient practice which in many cases has had a deep and sacred taproot in spiritual belief and ancestor worship. It is said that in some cases the accusation of cannibalism was used by European invaders to justify the genocide or enslavement of the peoples they encountered; the word 'cannibalism' is a garbled version of the name Caribbean, the home of the Carib tribes who were said to practise it.

'Endocannibalism' is the eating of the flesh of a loved one or member of the tribe to honour them and to keep their essence within the tribe, to make them *part of* their tribe in perpetuity, rather than losing them to the grave or pyre. Appalling as this may seem to 21st-century sensibilities, it was a deeply sacred act, and a very loving one, rooted in grief and honour for the deceased. In some cultures, the body was roasted and eaten like any other meat; in others it was burned and the ashes mixed with other foodstuffs before consumption by the family or the tribe. In some tribes, a single act of cannibalism was necessary on the death of the chief to transfer his leadership qualities, his courage and wisdom, to his successor. Unfortunately, the consumption of some tissues, including the brain, could lead to the transmission of disease to the consumers, such as tuberculosis and particularly the degenerative disease kuru, which, like Bovine Spongiform Encephalopathy, is acquired by eating infected material, the infection then migrating to the brain and central nervous system.

'Exocannibalism', which refers to the eating of people outside of one's community or tribe, may have had an exactly opposite motive and have been a means of utterly destroying or humiliating an enemy, a final and irreversible subjugation. The practice may involve only selected parts, such as the heart and liver, which might have been believed to transfer the courage and vital energy of the slain enemy to those who consumed him.

Some cannibalism was linked to religious practice: the Aztecs famously practised human sacrifice at their temple centre, Tenochtitlan, where the remains of many thousands of people have been found by archaeologists, and these bodies were eaten as sacred food – as part of the ritual.

Perhaps the most tragic instances of cannibalism are those where starving people are forced, against their strongest inclinations, to eat human flesh as a necessity for survival during extreme famine or in circumstances such as the Andes plane crash of 1972, in which the survivors were obliged to consume flesh taken from the bodies of those who had died on impact. They managed to survive for over two months in extreme weather conditions; what the psychological aftermath may have been, for them and the relatives of the deceased, is another matter. History is replete with examples of people who have been forced into this situation as a result of siege or famine.

It is relatively certain that cannibalism plays no major role in any culture's tradition today, yet it still takes place. In the 20th century, the Black author and anthropologist Zora Neale Hurston described cannibalism as still taking place in Haiti as part of Voodoo *Cochon Grise* traditions – some websites think it continues today. Certain serial killers have been known to eat parts of their victims, including Andrei Chikatilo, Jeffrey Dahmer, Albert Fish, Fritz Haarmann, Issei Sagama, and in this decade, Jason Thornburg. In a letter received by George Lusk, chairman of the Whitechapel Vigilance Committee in 1888, the writer, who claimed to be Jack the Ripper, said he had fried and eaten half of a kidney from the body of one of his victims, Catherine Eddowes. Her body had indeed been despoiled of a kidney, and half a decomposing kidney was enclosed with the note, which the unfortunate Lusk opened at the breakfast table. The Leopard Men of Sierra Leone, a criminal organisation that roughly aligned with the gangsters of 1920s America, demanded a human being to eat from anyone wishing to join them until the middle of the 20th century. The Ugandan dictator Idi Amin, who died in Saudi Arabia in 2003, allegedly left human remains behind in his fridge when he fled the country in 1979, and there is strong evidence that he practised cannibalism on top of his other human rights violations. Japanese officers are also said to have cannibalised Allied prisoners of war during World War II. And even today this horror seems to continue. Only a decade ago, ISIS soldiers were accused of forcing or tricking Yazidi people, members of a Kurdish race who were living in northern Iraq, to eat human flesh, including that of their own children – just one of many atrocities ISIS has committed there and elsewhere.

Medical cannibalism has been widespread in history, with the Ancient Greeks believing that human blood could cure epilepsy and many human body parts being used in traditional Chinese medicine, though in some cases these were things that did not cause the death of the donor, such as hair and fingernails. In 17th-century Europe, powdered human mummy – there was a brisk westward trade in Egyptian mummies – was a recognised cure for stomach problems and fits.

Okay, and that's enough of that. Brrrr.

CHAPTER THREE

# Food of the Gods

"Let's carve him as a dish fit for the gods,
Not hew him as a carcase fit for hounds."

– Shakespeare: *Julius Caesar*.

While humans have been engrossed by the search for, the preparation of and the consumption of food, even the Gods have not been exempt from this preoccupation – in the eyes of their adherents, at least. Christians today tend not to imagine their God sitting down to a hearty ploughman's and a tankard of beer in Heaven, but many people of older and current religions clearly gave a great deal of thought to how their Gods were nourished. Sacrifices of meat, bread and wine were all a part of this concern from the very earliest times as human spirituality developed. On Mount Olympus, Zeus and the other Gods and Goddesses were fed on ambrosia and drank nectar – magical substances which also ensured immortality and eternal youth and beauty for the Gods. Nectar is generally associated with honey, but ambrosia is an unknown, though it appears to have been imagined as a liquid that could be poured over someone. Both foods were brought to the Gods' dinner table by magical doves. However, they also benefited from the smoke of burnt sacrifices from their temples – although they were only offered the bones, skin and fat from any slaughtered animals, so it was as well they were also believed to enjoy the meat itself, which was eaten by the priests as part of the ritual.

The self-refilling cooking pot is a common theme in mythologies, deriving no doubt from the hunger of the early storytellers. In Irish legend, the Cauldron of the Dagda – one of the Four Treasures of the Tuatha de Danaan – provides an unending supply of food and drink which magically satisfies anyone who tastes it, without needing to have any ingredients put into it. The Norse Gods also went in for magical artefacts and animals, and in the home of the Gods and the glorious dead, Valhalla, a supernatural boar called 'Saehrimnir' provided a pork lunch every day. He was cooked in a special cauldron called 'Eldhrimnir' yet was always found running around, alive and well in the grounds of Valhalla by the evening, ready to be eaten again the next day. The God Thor also possessed two goats called 'Tanngrisnir' and 'Tanngnjóstr', who worked a day job as well as providing a continually renewable supper: they pulled his chariot but were killed and eaten every night, returning to life afterwards to be harnessed or eaten again. Not much of a life! Like the Olympians, the Norse Gods also needed to be kept young and healthy by magical means, and this was achieved by the actions of a Goddess called Idunn, who grew magical apples in her orchard and brought them to the Gods every day; when she was kidnapped by a giant in one story and the apples were no longer delivered, the Gods began to age. In China too, the Gods were only immortal because of some special peaches, which were grown in the gardens of Ximangwu, the Goddess of the western heavens, and only fruited once every millennium. When they did ripen, they were served at a special banquet to keep the Gods young and immortal. The Aztec Gods, as we have seen, needed human sacrifice, for they ate human flesh and drank human blood to keep their immortal state.

However, not all religions past and present have practised blood sacrifice. In Hindu temples, the food offered is generally vegetarian fare, in line with the principles of *Ahimsa*, the concept of living without injuring other creatures. The food, drink and flowers are offered to the Gods, but when they are believed to have taken the essence of the sacrifice, the food, now blessed by the Gods, is given to the worshippers as *prasada*, a practice which has become an important community meal in Hindu temples. This practice is also common to Sikhism. In Hinduism also the Gods rely on their special foods for their immortality: the Elixir of Wisdom consumed by the Gods and others is a combination of two magical liquids, *Amrita* and *Soma*, which between them give immortality, wisdom and inspiration.

The Gods of Ancient Egypt did not seem to need an elixir to maintain their divine immortality, yet they too benefited from sacrifices made to them in the temples, food which was later eaten by the priests. Ancient wall paintings and other art show that the meat was generally offered ready slaughtered and cut into joints, rather than as a blood sacrifice. Meat, either beef or hunted game, fowls such as geese and ducks (chickens were not commonly kept until the late period in Ancient Egypt) and their eggs, cakes and bread, honey, mead, beer and wine were offered, as well as flowers, although sacrifices were usually tailored to the God to whom they were being given, so that wine and sweets were offered to Bast, the Goddess of pleasure; the infant Horus was offered milk; the grain Goddess Renenut was offered cereals, and the lioness Goddess Sekhmet would be offered beer coloured with red ochre, as in the legend in which she began destroying mankind until placated with a lake of beer coloured to look like blood. The Egyptian priests took their physical care of the deities a step further, and the statues of the Gods in their shrines would be tended daily, being washed, scented, bedecked with jewellery and dressed in clean clothes before being offered their meals.

In modern Voodoo, food of all kinds, but especially meat and alcohol, are offered to the Orishas or Loas (a Loa is less than a god but more than a spirit). Most of the Loas have their own preferences: Damballa enjoys white foods such as rice, coconut, milk and water, while Baron Samedi likes rum, black coffee and spicy foods like chillis. Erzulie, who has at least two aspects, is offered food accordingly: to Erzulie Dantor, the warrior form, pork and rum are offered, while Erzulie Freda, the love Goddess, likes sweets of all kinds, as well as jewellery and perfume. Black cockerels, black dogs and black goats are also commonly sacrificed as part of Voodoo rituals.

Sacrificial offerings targeted at a particular deity could become quite complicated: in India, the Goddesses of night and sunrise may be offered milk … but it has to be the milk of a black cow who is mother to a white calf – the symbolism clearly being the light of the moon or dawn coming forth from darkness.

Worshippers of the Greek Goddess/Titan Hecate laid out suppers at crossroads, which were sacred to her, on the Deipnon, the night of the dark moon. These offerings included strong-smelling foods like garlic and onions and were meant as an offering to the hungry dead but were no doubt eaten by the poor. Modern pagans often continue this practice with 'Hecate suppers' and may donate to the poor, at a food bank, for example, on the appropriate date in Hecate's name.

Often the creatures being sacrificed were the sacred animals of the God to whom they were being offered. In Ancient Greece, it was common to offer bulls to Poseidon and male animals, bulls, rams, boars and he-goats to male Gods, especially those connected with fertility. The Ancient Egyptians offered rams to Amun, who was ram-headed, and cattle to cow-headed Hat-Hor, and in later times mummies of these and other animals were offered. Thousands of cat mummies, created to honour the Goddess Bast, have been found at her temple in Bubastis, Egypt. The Norsemen offered pork and boars to the fertility God Freyr, to whom they were sacred, and it was customary in Greece to sacrifice black dogs to Hecate for the same reason.

Zoroastrianism, an ancient religion that was well-established long before Christianity, once required the sacrifice of living animals, as well as other foodstuffs, such as bread, milk, and nectar derived from the Haoma plant, a woody gymnosperm species. However, in modern Zoroastrian practice, the killing of animals is no longer considered appropriate, and the usual offerings are simply bread, milk and nectar.

The Incas sacrificed alpacas, llamas and guinea pigs, while the Mayans offered a huge variety of animals from deer and dogs to wild predators, such as alligators and jaguars, which must have been challenging to capture alive and subdue for the ritual. In Northern Europe the Samis sacrificed the reindeer, which is an animal vital to their culture and way of life even today.

Ancient Judaism approved animal sacrifice, which is mentioned in several Bible stories, including the mass slaughter of animals at the dedication of Solomon's Temple and Abel's offering of sheep, which was more acceptable to Yahweh than the fruits and vegetables offered by his brother Cain. In one of the crueller Bible stories, Abraham was made aware that he was expected to sacrifice his son Isaac … until God relented and sent a ram in his place at the last moment. And this tradition has been carried on by some Christians, who still practise animal sacrifice to this day. Although it has never been part of general Christian practices, some strains of Greek and Armenian Orthodox Christianity kill an animal, commonly a bovine, on certain feast days. The meat is then shared among the community.

And speaking of Christianity, in some religions the God may himself be sacrificed! Christians believe Jesus sacrificed himself for mankind, and in the Catholic eucharist, the communion wafer (bread) and wine are believed to become the body and blood of Jesus (transubstantiation) and are consumed as such. In Aztec practice, the sun God Huitzilopochtli was himself eaten by his followers in the form of a shape made from vegetable matter and human blood, which was ceremonially pronounced to be Huitzilopochtli before being cut into pieces and eaten as part of the ritual. In Mithraism the divine bull was sacrificed by Mithras (although he was not eaten) in order that the universe might be constructed from his body and blood (several belief paths have a large creature or person being killed in order that its body might be used to create the physical world). In Ancient Egyptian tombs, Osiris corn beds were sometimes placed – these were a wooden outline of the God (instantly recognisable for his mummy shape and

*Atef* headdress), which was filled with mud and sprinkled with cereal seeds, which were then watered. In the tomb, this would germinate. However, archaeologists believe the bed was placed for the symbolism of resurrection, rather than as food.

Food may also play a part in traditions around honouring and mourning the dead. Probably the cult of the dead in Ancient Egypt is the best-known example. It was a major preoccupation of this ancient civilisation, which spent enormous amounts of wealth and manpower in the creation of arguably the most impressive and long-lasting tombs in the world. As with the Gods, food sacrifices were made in the funerary chapels associated with the tombs, though food may well have been offered at the graves of even the most lowly peasants and artisans. Egyptian belief included the need to provide for the dead person in the afterlife, so preparations for a deceased pharaoh would have been considerable – and don't forget he was also considered to be a God himself, so there was a religious side to the offerings, as well as honour and grief. Tutankhamen was provided with choice cuts of beef, geese, ducks and wild fowls, all carefully mummified, as well as sealed containers of grains for making bread in the afterlife (don't worry: the king had his own magical servants there in the form of carved *shabtis* to do all his work for him!), as well as baskets of fruit (some ready-stoned), honey, vegetables and spices, and seeds to grow more. Tutankhamen, a minor Pharaoh with a stain on his lineage as the son of the hated 'heretic king' Akhenaton, was only 19 when he died, and yet his treasures have caused jaws to drop across the world since 1922. Imagine the scale of the burial goods Rameses the Great took to the afterlife with him!

These supplies were meant to last the dead man for all eternity, so as time passed, the priests came up with ingenious ways of ensuring he never ran out of necessities, including painting glowing pictures of the food on the tomb walls – magically, these would work just as well as the preserved real food – and even writing the names of food on the walls to the same purpose.

Figs, olives and other fruits were interred with the dead in Ancient Greece, along with wine, milk, honey, oil, and even water. The food left with the deceased would also include a piece of cake or bread to be thrown to Cerberus, the monstrous three-headed dog who guarded the gates of Hades, so that the dead person might slip past while the dog snapped up his treat – we still use the expression 'a sop to Cerberus' today, meaning a small gesture to someone unpleasant or difficult, to smooth the way. The offerings continued regularly for the first year after the funeral and thereafter once a year. The importance of these offerings to the dead is mentioned by Homer, who also describes magical offerings of blood, oil, wine, milk, and honey poured into a trench to conjure the dead. In one grisly passage in *The Odyssey*, Odysseus digs such a trench to conjure the spirit of Tiresias to ask his advice on getting home, cutting the throats of sheep and goats over the trench to fill it with blood and keeping away other spirits who show themselves until the blind prophet has drunk his fill.

In Ancient Rome, burial feasts were included in the grave accessories, but offerings would continue to be made by family members. Some graves had a tube installed that could be used to pour offerings into the tomb from above … not much good for solid food, though.

In many ancient cultures, the food offered to the dead was actually consumed by the funeral attendees, usually as a sort of picnic around the grave or in the funerary temple. In mediaeval Germany, bread was mixed, and the dough might be laid on the deceased person's body in the open coffin to rise, as it was believed some of the essence or spirit of the dead person might enter the bread…an echo of earlier cannibalistic practices meant to keep the dead person in the tribe.

The Ancient Chinese took this idea a step further and prepared funeral cakes to be eaten by 'sin-eaters', monks who would thus take the dead person's sins, committed during their lifetime, upon themselves. The Chinese also honoured their dead with food and still do so today. If the deceased was a rich person, his body would be sealed with jade tiles to prevent corruption, and special paper money was sent with him into the next world (by burning) to ensure his comfort there. This *joss* money is a tradition that continues today, and it is used with incense and food offerings to the deceased. Coins – real money – are also offered to guests at the funeral for good luck. Funeral homes in China usually offer a funeral meal for the attendees – a custom we in the West would recognise as a wake.

The wake, by this and other names, is an almost universal custom arising out of the need to care for guests who may have come a long distance for the funeral, although the wake could also be a vigil (staying *awake*) held with the body before the burial or cremation – which is where it gets its Western name. The British sherry-and-ham-sandwich tea may have come a long way from earlier, more elaborate customs, but it has the same origin and reason. Generally, there are levels of attendance at a funeral, with only close family and friends being 'invited back' to the home of the deceased, or a nearby relative's, for the meal.

In some places, notably Wales and some regions of the US, the food is generally prepared and brought to the home by caring neighbours, with the thinking that the recently bereaved might be in no state to make food and should not have this additional worry at such a time. Some better-off families might take this thinking a step further and hold the wake at an hotel or restaurant.

The choice of funeral foods is a whole other subject. Hindus avoid meat (if they do not do so normally) so that the deceased may attain salvation. The old tradition of funeral cakes goes back many centuries in Britain; the cakes usually being marked with a cross or other symbol. Soul cakes, a similar idea, were once prepared at Halloween and were given to people who called at the home of the bereaved family and offered prayers for the soul of the dead person.

Finally, long after the death of the person, customs that include food and drink may continue in many traditions, from the simple raising of a glass of wine as a toast to them at Christmas or the deceased person's birthday to the various festivals of the dead around the world. In Britain, we hardly think of the beloved dead at Halloween, yet this ancient festival, now eclipsed by children's games and American practices, was once the Celtic time for honouring – and fearing – the dead. It continues under several guises in the UK: in Wales it is *Nos Calan Gaeaf*, on the Isle of Man *Hop-tu-Naa*, in Cornwall *Kalan Gwav*. The festival was *liminal*: an important distinction for the Celts, who saw boundaries – between times or places – as magical. Halloween (or rather, *Samhain*) was not only celebrated at sundown on the last day of one month and sunrise on the first day of the next but was also considered the boundary between the old year and the new. Christians, especially Catholics, celebrate All Saints' Day and All Souls' Day on 1st and 2nd November, respectively, although these can be considered to be a Christianising of existing Celtic practices as a way of stamping out paganism.

While pagans may still observe these practices with solemn rituals to remember the ancestors at Samhain, non-pagans generally see it as a bit of fun, something for children, a time to tell ghost stories around the fire – and eat a lot of chocolate. Trick-or-treating in spooky costumes for the children goes back to an ancient belief that a disguise was necessary at this time in case evil entities or the spirits of angry ancestors who had not been remembered or treated well were abroad. Now it is an opportunity for the children to proffer their bags and be given sweet treats, often in 'spooky' shapes: bat-shaped cookies and cupcakes with icing spiders on them. Many confectioners sell gruesome or spooky sweets, such as gummy snakes, 'eyeballs', chocolate ghosts, and chocolate spiders in the run-up to this festival. Dark, spiced foods like gingerbread and dark toffee, and spicy drinks like cider cup, are also traditional at this time. But suppers are also associated with Halloween, with the pumpkin playing a starring role in these as pumpkin soup, pumpkin muffins and pumpkin pie, utilising the flesh of the gourds that have been hollowed out to use as pumpkin lanterns. The now familiar large orange pumpkin arrived here in the UK from the US but has been accepted as a vital part of this festival, and even its colour has become a part of the scene, with food (such as cupcakes, cookies, and sweets) often coloured black and orange. The more traditional British apple still appears as pies, cakes and toffee-apples; once it played a vital and magical role at Halloween, with young girls tossing its peel over their shoulders in a small magical ritual to see who they would marry, or sleeping with the fruit under their pillows to dream of their future husbands, and people ducking or bobbing for apples at parties and fairs. The apples were also buried at crossroads and other locations for the sustenance of spirits who had no families remaining to look after them, and food was left on doorsteps for the dead. In more recent times, pagans may hold 'dumb suppers' at Samhain to honour the ancestors and the more recent beloved dead, eating the entire meal in total silence whilst thinking of those who have passed away and even inviting them to the table and laying places for them (see Chapter Nine).

Dia de los Muertes, the famous Mexican festival of the dead, held a couple of days after Halloween, famously features edible sugar skulls, although the festival has to some extent moved on from ancestor worship to become a colourful time of fun more akin to carnival. In India, for *Sraddha*, Hindu families offer food, especially rice, to the dead on the anniversary of their passing to ensure they are peaceful and well-provided for in the afterlife. There is also an annual festival lasting 16 days called Pitru Paksha at which these customs are enacted. Crows are sacred to this practice, and food is offered to them as well. Taoists and Buddhists in Asia also make food offerings to their departed relatives at the Hungry Ghost Festival in September, where lighted lanterns are also set afloat on waterways for luck. On Nine-Nights in the Caribbean, families share food to honour the dead, eating and drinking together while sharing memories for the nine days of the festival. Native American customs include offering food, typically cornmeal and foods made with cornmeal, into a 'spirit dish' for the ancestors to enjoy.

CHAPTER FOUR

# Food for the Land

> "Food is everything we are. It's an extension of nationalist feeling, ethnic feeling, your personal history, your province, your region, your tribe, your grandma."
>
> – Anthony Bourdain.

Quietly the elderly woman pushes open the wooden door and steps outside, carefully holding a pottery saucer filled with fresh milk in her work-worn hands. Stooping, she lays the dish on the edge of the stone doorstep, then straightens up, wiping her hands in her rough sacking apron.

"Bless this house and all within; bring no harm to me or my kin," she mutters, afraid lest her husband should hear her 'pagan nonsense' and come out to rebuke her. Yet this practice is one she has carried out every night of her married life, through thin times and times of plenty, believing always that the goodwill and blessings of the Fae have at all times kept her from the worst.

'Libation' is a term meaning the offering of a food or drink as a sacrifice to gods or spirits as part of a ritual. It generally refers to liquids, but solid foods can also be libated. Generally, the liquid is poured directly on to the altar or the ground and may consist of wine, beer, cider, honey, oil, milk, or even water. People have always recognised that there are supernatural forces in the landscape, spirits and beings who may need propitiating if humans are to live and farm there without problems. Primarily, offerings were left out or placed somewhere special for protection, to incur the goodwill of these beings so that they did no harm and might even actively shield the inhabitants from evil and ill fortune, and this particularly applied to homes.

Many an owner of an old house has found unusual objects in the walls and foundations of his building, perhaps when alterations or repairs are being carried out. The Museum of Witchcraft and Magic in Boscastle, Cornwall, has a couple of gruesome mummified cats, which would have been walled up (hopefully not still alive) for magical reasons, perhaps to keep down mice and rats. Shoes are another common inclusion. The most common offerings in walls and foundations are coins, but food has also been found as an offering to local spirits to protect the building and its inhabitants. Typically, the food is in a container, such as a jar of honey, but more perishable items may have been included and simply not left any perceptible remains.

People on farms in the UK and Ireland have traditionally left out food or drink for the fairies, a practice that continues today among the superstitious and among magical practitioners. Milk and cream have always been the favoured choice: this would be partly to dissuade the Fair Folk from causing mischief in the dairy, spoiling or stealing the produce, and partly to seek their help with the work. Butter churning is a difficult process, particularly in hot weather; the farmer might drop a silver or gold coin into the churn if the process was taking more time than it should, and the belief was that the fairies could help or hinder this according to their disposition towards the dairy owner – or just their mood (the fairies of historical belief were a long way removed from the sanitised, glitter-clad Tinker

Bells of modern children's entertainment). Honey, bread, cake, and alcoholic drink are also considered appropriate for the fairies. The practice might also be believed to keep the fairies from stealing children – newborn babies – and substituting their own in their place. In Scotland, the brownie (a sort of *Dobby the House Elf*) was believed to come at night and perform tasks around the home to help, and food might be left out in gratitude. My own mother, who was born in 1930 of partly Irish stock and was deeply superstitious, used always to leave a portion of food on her plate, which we teasingly accused her of setting aside "for the brownie". She never denied it!

Supernatural creatures might also be induced to help in the home as a workplace, a theme that the Brothers Grimm explored in their tale of *the Elves and the Shoemaker*, in which a poor shoemaker finds his fortunes taking an upturn when three benevolent elves come to his home at night and finish his shoes for him. In this story, the *libation* is not food but suits of clothes for the elves who have made him rich. Beatrix Potter used this same theme in her children's book *The Tailor of Gloucester*, in which mice show their gratitude for being rescued by the cat by finishing a costly coat for an important customer for their host. Potter's story had its origins in a real local event where a man known to her had claimed the fairies had come to assist him with his work.

Leaving food out as offerings for 'spirits' is a well-known phenomenon across almost all cultures, with the food being left as an inducement to bring good fortune to the household or the community – or at least refrain from doing it harm. Each culture has its own traditions around the practice.

In Thailand, food and other offerings are left in small red-painted 'spirit houses' either adjacent to homes or on streets and in corners everywhere. The goods are left for the spirits, including the recent dead and ancestors.

In India, live cobras are kept in temples and other public places as sacred animals and are offered milk and ghee (clarified butter) at festivals – purely ceremonial, as they can neither lap up the milk nor digest it. The Hindu sacred cows also receive food at festivals and at other times and are even cared for in special shelters, with food and veterinary care, when they become too old to scavenge for themselves.

In many cases, sacred places in the landscape were marked, perhaps by an ancient and sacred tree or grove or perhaps by a carefully constructed and aligned ring of stones or a single standing stone, and it is certain that sacrifices would have been made at these places, either offerings of food and drink or sacrifices of living animals or even of people. While no evidence of human sacrifice has been found at Stonehenge, despite its so-called 'slaughter stone', a great deal of items have been excavated which indicate that food offerings or ritual communal meals took place there: bones, mostly from pigs but also from cattle; fruit seeds and other vegetable remains; and pieces of cookery pots. These were also found at nearby Woodhenge and the more recently excavated Durrington Walls, though archaeologists feel human sacrifices may have been carried out at Woodhenge.

Sacred trees and groves were used by the Druids for worship, and historical sources mention human sacrifices taking place, with the bodies of the victims being hung on the trees. Food sacrifices and libations of ale and wine may also have formed a part of these rituals. Many trees were associated in the Celtic tradition with the Otherworld, particularly trees which bear white flowers and red or dark red berries, and food offerings would have been laid under these, as well as outside the home, to please the Fae or other spirits of the region. In India, the peepal (a species of fig), banyan, and jujube trees are sacred to several faiths, including Hinduism, Jainism, Buddhism and Sikhism, and offerings are made to them at festivals and other times, often of their own fruit! Sacred groves are also celebrated in a similar manner in India. In Africa, the baobab tree, a giant fruiting tree with a bulbous trunk, is believed to be the home of the spirits of ancestors and is given offerings of food that the ancestors may enjoy. Ancestors or other spirits may also inhabit trees in Japanese Shinto belief, and offerings of food, flowers and other items may be made at the tree's foot or at a nearby shrine. In Korea, certain trees are believed to protect the village from evil spirits and other perils and are given offerings in gratitude.

Offering the sacred trees parts of their own fruits is also seen today in Britain in the ancient custom of wassailing, in which a group of people, often in ritual costume, visits the apple orchard in winter and greets the trees with traditional words and song, toasting them with cider made from their fruits and pouring some at the roots of each tree or hanging a piece of bread or toast soaked in cider in their branches. The people carrying out the ritual typically have drums and other noisemakers with them – and may even fire shotguns – for the purpose of scaring away any evil spirits who may wish to harm the trees or steal their fruit.

The fertility of the land was of vital importance to our forebears, who had of course no way of ordering a hundred sacks of nitrogen fertiliser from online agri-stores but had to rely on their own methods involving the sweepings of the cowshed and stables and their own religious practices to earn the goodwill of the spirits and deities of the land. One common practice was the offering of 'first fruits' – the very first things harvested in the season were offered to the Gods or the spirits of the land; even today, these are brought to church for 'Harvest Festival', in which local communities and schools may also be involved and may afterwards be given to charity or to the poor via food banks and organisations for the homeless. In Tudor times, in some regions of the UK, land was left untilled for the spirits of the region to grow their own crops (in Scotland, this is referred to as 'Goodman's or Guideman's land'), and long after this practice was outlawed by the Church and made impossible by heavy tithing, small areas of grain were left at the edges and corners of the fields for the spirits or for the poor to come gleaning after the main harvest was done.

In Cornwall and other regions, 'Crying the Neck' is still performed at the end of the harvest. The farmer is careful to leave the very last sheaf uncut in the centre of the field, and this becomes the focus of the ritual, with the farmer or other celebrant ceremonially cutting the sheaf and holding it up to the east, then the south, then the west, in token of the sun's passage across the sky while crying, "I have 'un! I have 'un! I have 'un!" There is a traditional set of responses from the gathered crowd, all involving a lot of shouting, noise and fun, after which they all go off and gather for a communal meal … once, this would have included offerings of food and drink to the land itself.

In Japan, the autumn Tsukimi Festival includes the offering of nuts and beans and a communal feast of rice balls and other traditional foods, although this celebration is themed on the moon rather than the land.

Although the festival of Thanksgiving is held in many countries across the world, in the US it is a celebration of national identity as well as a harvest festival, dating back to an event in 1621 when the first settlers had survived a very hard winter which had killed half of their number. They celebrated with a three-day festival; the food supposedly being shared with members of the Native American community. Today, Americans still dress up in 17th-century costume and get together for family meals, typically including turkey and pumpkin pie (as we have seen, the pumpkin has also become deeply associated with Halloween on either side of the 'pond').

In ancient times, blood sacrifice would have been more usual at harvest time, but food and drink were also offered. In Greece, food sacrifices such as cakes and liquid sacrifices such as wine, milk, and oil were buried in trenches as an offering to the land – as opposed to the ritual burning which would send offerings upwards towards the Gods. The Romans were more inclined to make animal sacrifices, but often components of the animal might be seasoned and prepared as dishes to be offered by burning. The Suovitaurilia sacrifice, which was aimed specifically at blessing and purifying the land, might include leading a ram, a boar and a bull around the fields before sacrificing them at a public occasion (in the event of a piece of private land being blessed, juvenile animals – a lamb, a piglet and a calf – would be used). In Ancient China, the She-Ji deities (She = 'soil' and Ji = 'grain') were offered food, wine, flowers, and often animal sacrifices in large state rituals, as the fertile land was considered the most important element of the nation's wellbeing, but offerings of food and drink would also be made in other places to propitiate the protective spirits of the place so that they might bless households and people. In modern times, the Chinese still offer food, wine, flowers, incense, and paper money to the land, laying the offerings at temples, shrines, or at the graves of family members.

In Britain and Europe, the Celts were more likely to offer precious metal objects or weapons, but they also presented foodstuffs such as oats, salt and herbs to the spirits of the land and to water deities of rivers and the sea. The Norsemen also offered weapons, typically beautiful swords which have been retrieved from peat bogs and lakes, but they also left honey, bread, fruits, and drink at simple forest or moorland altars made of rocks for the spirits of the land.

Offerings made into rivers and other larger bodies of water were also common, although the most frequent types of sacrifices found are metal objects such as jewellery and swords – which would be ritually broken before being given to the water, presumably to prevent anyone sneaking back afterwards and diving for them! In Ancient Egypt, jars of beer were poured into the Nile to thank Father Haapi for the inundation which flooded the Nile valley with the rich alluvial soil needed to grow crops, as well as the water which, as long as it lasted, was carried through the farmlands by means of a system of ditches and *shaduf* (a simple crane-type device for lifting water from one level to another). In Ancient Greece, bulls and horses might have been offered to the sea as Poseidon, but it was more common for the offerings to be liquids such as beer, wine, and milk. In many cultures, pure water was often offered to the sea or to rivers and lakes as a way of thanking the water spirits for their gift of life.

In modern pagan practice, libation is an important part of the ritual and usually takes place towards the end, when a communion-like sharing of cakes and wine forms one of the last actions before the circle is opened or the sacred place is left. In Wicca, small cakes are blessed by the high priestess before being passed around from one person to another with a kiss and a blessing, typically "May you never hunger." Then the high priestess and high priest together bless the wine, and this is also passed around with the words, "May you never thirst" (once this would have been in a large altar chalice, but since the Covid pandemic, most covens and other pagan groups prefer individuals to bring their own cups). This small ritual ends with a cake and a splash of wine being offered in a libation bowl, or simply dropped on to the ground by the altar if the ritual is outdoors. The words that accompany this offering may vary from a simple "Accept this offering" to a complex speech honouring the ancestors, asking for protection or blessings, or thanking the Gods: "for flags, flax, fodder, and frig" (for a roof over one's head, clothes to wear, food to eat, and someone to bed with) is a fairly common one for gratitude.

Modern Druids offer their own homegrown produce and herbs, or natural foods they have bought, which are placed on the altar at the start of the ritual and will be left behind afterwards as long as no bones or plastic wrappers are included. In Heathenry and Asatru (a modern pagan stream which honours the Norse Gods), an offering is called a 'blót' and may consist of any sort of natural food (as opposed to supermarket-wrapped factory food) and alcohol, typically mead or beer, offered to the land in a responsible way, without non-degradable wrappings, on a flat rock or at the foot of a tree.

The leaving of food which has been ritually offered is – or should be – always done thoughtfully and carefully by modern pagans, who are careful not to leave any food that could cause health problems for wild animals or birds or to leave any litter. With indoor rituals, the libations may be composted or even – in the event the host does not have a garden – put in the rubbish bin, as the Gods and spirits are believed to have already benefited from it through the mere act of giving.

Many modern pagans make a practice of visiting sacred sites such as holy wells, standing stones and stone circles, and ancient trees, and will leave libations of drink and offerings of food, generally 'natural' food such as fruits, nuts and seeds, chosen for their suitability for the local wildlife, as well as flowers and leaves, at these sites. Again, such practitioners are generally careful never to leave material behind that is not biodegradable: even paper used in the ritual may be gathered up and taken away, although rice paper may have been substituted. Our forebears may have left more enduring offerings such as stones, shells, coins, and 'clooties' – small strips of cloth left tied to branches. However, modern pagans are more aware of the environmental sensitivity of such sites and will generally ensure clooties are made from natural materials such as wool and cotton and that nothing durable is left behind. The exception is the ongoing practice of dropping coins into wells and other – usually manmade – small bodies of water, which is done by pagans and non-pagans alike, often with a wish or a prayer for a person now in spirit. Or the well may be in a conserved location where the coins may be retrieved at intervals to help pay for the upkeep of the site.

CHAPTER FIVE

# The Food of Folklore

"Food, culture, people, and landscape are inseparably linked."

– Anthony Bourdain.

As a child, I was an avid reader of the weekly comic books *The Beano* and *The Dandy*. Even then, I was struck by a curious and recurring theme: an almost comical preoccupation with food. The characters – though more accurately, the artists behind them – seemed to have an obsession with it. Almost every escapade ended with the heroes grinning from ear to ear, clutching newspaper packs of fish and chips, or being rewarded with towering, iced fruit cakes (always crowned with a solitary cherry), ice creams or bulging bags of sweets. Published by Dundee-based DC Thomson from the mid-1930s, these comics found their greatest success in a time when hunger was a real and pressing concern for many in Scotland. Perhaps that is why food loomed so large in their pages – not merely as a treat, but as a symbol of triumph, comfort, and joy. After all, food is one of humanity's most primal preoccupations. It threads through our songs and stories, our rituals and rewards, second only to romantic love in its emotional resonance, and in children's literature it often takes the place of love and sex, concepts which are not considered suitable for young minds.

A look through the mentions of food and feasting in our ancient folklore demonstrates to us not only this preoccupation but also the poverty of the people who created the stories in the past. Why do the Three Bears get so angry at poor Goldilocks for eating their porridge? Maybe if she'd nicked a haunch of beef or a freshly-baked fruitcake ... but porridge? But of course, the diet of the ancient poor (and the story is almost certainly a lot older than its first publication by Robert Southey) largely consisted of such stodge. Mediaeval peasants lived mainly on cereal porridges and pottage made from vegetables, so the loss of a bowl of porridge might cause them actual hardship.

Often food – like sex and love – should be treated with suspicion in mythologies and folk tales, for it could be a deadly trap. Persephone, abducted and forcibly married by the God of the underworld, Hades, is tracked down by her mother, Demeter, who demands of the Gods that her daughter be returned. But Persephone has eaten six pomegranate seeds – an oddly specific number – in the underworld and so cannot return permanently, though Zeus brokers a deal in which she can go back to mum for half the year (the Ancient Greek explanation for the changing seasons). This idea of forbidden foods also appears in the Christian Bible as the *Fruit of the Tree of Knowledge* (usually depicted or described as an apple) eaten by Adam and Eve after God had forbidden them to eat from the tree. The consequence is that they are thrown out of Eden.

Another consequence of eating magical foods is that one might lose touch with one's own life. On the isle of the Lotus Eaters in Greek mythology, those who ate of the magical flowers – if that is what they were – forgot their real lives and entered a fugue state so that they never left the island.

The Lethe, a river in the underworld, had the same powers, so that the dead who drank of it on their way through forgot their lives on earth, while in Japan eating Yomotsu-hegui, the fruit of hell, will give the eater immortality but keep them trapped there forever.

These ideas go on into more recent stories, where food and drink may be magical. People taken by the fairies or those who wander into their realms on their own, like Childe Rowland, may lose their ability to return to the world of mortals if they consume food or drink there. Going by what transpires with other fairy gifts, they are better off not eating it in any case: fairy coins and other gifts have a way of turning into mouldy dead leaves or other unpleasant things after the 'glamour' placed upon them fades away. The food may also appear as a temptation in itself, a bait for a trap, such as the gingerbread cottage (what a picture that creates in a child's imagination!) that lures Hansel and Gretel into the witch's clutches. In many fairytales, the hero or heroine themselves may be in danger of becoming food, as Hansel is, though his cleverer sister gives him a chicken bone to hold out when the short-sighted witch comes to prod him to see if he is fat enough to eat yet – in these stories, witches are often portrayed as cannibals, particularly of children. In the rather convoluted tale of *Jack and the Beanstalk*, Jack climbs to another world and steals from a terrifying man-eating giant who threatens to "grind his bones to make my bread". Another popular example is *Red Riding Hood*, a girl who is stalked by a wolf who swallows her granny and dresses in the granny's clothes to lure the girl into its jaws. And in some stories, the danger of being eaten is only averted by the main character's verbal cunning, as in *The Three Billy Goats Gruff*, where the smallest of three goats, crossing the hungry troll's bridge, tells the monster that he is far too small to be worth eating, and the troll should wait for his bigger, fatter brothers. The middle brother then tells exactly the same tale: that the troll should wait for the biggest goat … who is actually a force to be reckoned with and butts the troll right off his own bridge! Fairytales were originally much darker than the sanitised versions found in children's books today and may have once been cautionary (or plain scary) tales for adults rather than for the nursery. The theme of humans as food, or even cannibalism, runs through many of them, echoing one of our deepest horrors: viz., the Grimm Brothers' tale, *The Gingerbread Man*, who despite being made of cake is clearly a sentient humanoid being bent on escaping the stomachs of his pursuers. Jung stated that the tales are filled with archetypes from our unconscious and that they allow adults as well as children to explore and even deal with their deepest buried fears within the comforting medium of a story.

In some stories, the magical food may cause the characters to bite off more than they can chew, as in *Alice's Adventures in Wonderland*, where she finds a series of little cakes and bottles of liquid, all marked 'eat me' or 'drink me'. Each time, the consumption of the food causes her to grow very tall or shrink away to the size of a mouse, and it is the giant mushroom that the Caterpillar sits on that proves to be the antidote ("one side will make you grow taller, the other will make you grow shorter," advises the sagacious larva). In C.S. Lewis's *The Lion, the Witch and the Wardrobe*, the boy Edmund is given magical Turkish delight by the wicked queen and loses his ability to do anything but obey her in hopes of getting more of the poisoned but addictive sweets. In Christina Rossetti's 19th-century magical poem-story, *Goblin Market*, a girl gives in to temptation and tries the fruit being hawked by the evil goblins – despite having been warned and despite having lost a sister to the poisoned fruit. As soon as she has tasted it, she begins to waste away in longing for the magical food … and the goblins have become invisible to her, so that she is only saved by a courageous action by her surviving sister … a more modern revisiting of the theme of fairy food as a danger, which, like the concept of taboo food, may trace back to actual poisoning through eating tainted or toxic food.

Finally, food may just be poisoned, like the shiny rosy apple offered to Snow White by her wicked stepmother, disguised as a harmless old lady. Food from fairyland may also prove fatally poisonous to humans who eat it. In an Indian tale, an unfortunate snake is to blame for the death of an old man, as its venom is accidentally spilt into a dish of rice which has been given to him in charity, as it is carried away by a bird of prey.

The various legends around fairy women and selkies – supernatural seal-women who can assume human form when they walk on dry land and return to their seal shape when they re-enter the water – can include the use of food to entice them by lovelorn landlubbers. In one story, a man tries to tempt a selkie (in some versions it's a fairy woman or a mermaid) with his mother's fresh-baked bread (strangely, not fish!), but she complains it is too hard for her. So he tries her with raw dough, and that doesn't go down well either. Finally, his mother half-bakes some bread so that it is warm and fragrant but still soft, and this compromise lures the Otherworld woman to come and be his wife.

Fairies and other supernatural creatures that enter the human world do not appear to be affected by the food they eat in the same way as humans who enter Fairyland. The ancient belief in *changelings* (fairy children left in exchange for human babies abducted by fairies) includes the information that these creatures are constantly ravenously hungry and will devour any food they can find, causing hardship and even starvation to the human family. Yet if the correct magical procedure is carried out, the afflicted parents can send back the changeling and even have their own child returned to them.

Young children's relationship with food can be problematic, as any parent will tell you, and this is reflected in children's literature to the present day. The idea of huge bubbling vats of chocolate and candy is celebrated in Roald Dahl's *Charlie and the Chocolate Factory*, a book from 60 years ago which is still popular and still generating film versions, long after the author's death. He also wrote *James and the Giant Peach* – another story which was inspired by the fantasy of being surrounded by delicious, sweet food. Less appetising and even older, Dr Seuss's *Green Eggs and Ham* explores the idea of new foods for children, who can be faddy and particular about things they are not accustomed to; many children's books explore the notion of revolting gustatory ideas (*The Disgusting Sandwich* picture book; *I Won't Eat That*; and *Ketchup on Cornflakes* – all for younger children). Sometimes the idea of another creature being the one doing the eating, perhaps a frightening and threatening one, is the theme, and two other older children's books, *The Tiger Who Came to Tea* and *The Very Hungry Caterpillar*, create light-hearted and repetitive stories out of this idea.

This naturally leads on to stories in which people are eaten, usually, but not always, by monsters or by natural predators, the terrors of the latter requiring no explanation. Many stories and folk tales include this happening to lesser characters in the story. Homer's *Odyssey*, for example, gives a terrifying – and often revolting – description of the Cyclops Polyphemus, a one-eyed giant, devouring Odysseus's men as part of his wine-soaked supper, and in *Beowulf*, one of the earliest pieces of English literature, the terrifying Grendel breaks into the King's hall by night and steals away men to eat under the waters of the lake in which he and his monstrous mother live. In the popular fairytale, Red Riding Hood's poor granny has already been swallowed by the Big Bad Wolf when the girl arrives at her cottage; though in some versions, the wolf is hacked open by the courageous woodsman who comes to the rescue, and granny emerges unscathed. The stealing of babies by monsters who eat them is a particularly horrible section of this type of belief, with examples such as Lamia (Ancient Greece), a demon who eats babies in revenge for the killing of her own children by Hera, her Mesopotamian and Hebrew counterpart Lilith, and the Slavic witch figure Baba Yaga, who will eat children and adults who come near her magical cottage, which struts about on chicken legs. These have given way in more recent times to the generic bogeyman, who is sometimes used in unenlightened cultures to frighten children into good behaviour. The bogeyman (or boogeyman in the US) typically lives under the child's bed or in the bedroom closet, from whence he will emerge to eat the child if it has misbehaved. These kinds of stories seem to come from the darkest part of our unconscious or our race memories of ancient predators and have made their way into all corners of our culture, from children's stories to the heraldry of modern companies (for example, the serpent swallowing a man motif on the Alfa Romeo car badge, drawn from the arms of the city of Milan).

A final and even more gruesome word on child-eating is the idea of being fed the flesh of one's own loved ones, or of any children, unsuspectingly. The Titan Cronus, father of the Gods, swallowed his own offspring as soon as they were born, until their mother Rhea broke the cycle by giving him a wrapped stone instead of the infant Zeus, but this was a deliberate act to hold on to his own power and position. In the German fairytale *The Juniper Tree* the wicked stepmother (aren't they always?) murders her stepson out of jealousy and makes soup from his body, which she feeds to his father. The mythical Phrygian King Tantalus tried to trick the Gods into eating the cooked flesh of his own son, Pelops, and was punished for it by being chained in a pool of water in Hades, a pool that receded every time he tried to drink from it; this idea gave us the name 'Tantalus' for a locked decanter of drinks and the word 'tantalise'. A similar Greek story told is of Lycaon, king of Arcadia, trying to feed his son to Zeus – who turned him into a wolf for his crimes. Atreus killed and cooked the young sons of his brother, Thyestes, and served the meat to him, afterwards showing him the heads and hands of the children to bring it home to him what he had just eaten. The reason for this was that Thyestes had had an affair with Atreus's wife. Continuing on the theme of forced cannibalism as punishment, Procne killed her own child and fed it to her husband Tereus, who had raped her sister and cut out her tongue to prevent her telling anyone.

Cannibalism is rarer in more modern literature, yet who can forget the cannibals in the classic story of *Robinson*

*Crusoe* – my childhood copy had some fairly gruesome colour illustrations as well – who is terrified when canoes full of 'savages' and prisoners arrive on his island for their version of a barbecue. To his even greater horror, Man Friday, who has escaped from the cannibals into his protection, suggests with gestures that they should eat the bodies after Crusoe has defeated the enemy.

However, although there are plenty of grisly legends about ghouls and other monsters who consume living people and corpses, there are forms of being eaten that are often considered worse than simple physical consumption and lead not only to the body being destroyed but sometimes the soul as well. Ammit (Eater of the Dead) is a chimaera in Ancient Egyptian mythology who devours the souls of those who fail the judgement before Osiris, meaning that they have lied to the 42 judges of the dead about the sins they committed during their lives. In Egyptian belief, the dead man was led past the judges, who each asked him whether he had committed a specific sin, and he was obliged to answer. Then his heart was weighed before Osiris against the feather of truth by Anubis, the God of the dead, while Thoth, the God of knowledge and wisdom, recorded the result. Should the heart outweigh the feather (even today we talk about people with clear consciences being 'light-hearted'), this monstrous Goddess – she had the head of a crocodile and a lion and hippopotamus body – wolfed down the sinner's soul, which presumably meant an end to him on all the planes of existence – the 'second death' so feared by the Ancient Egyptians. In Hindu folklore, the Rakshasa (female demons) are said to eat human flesh and even devour souls. In more modern mythology, a bite from a supernatural creature can lead to the loss of one's soul, as in the set of beliefs around vampires, who suck the blood from the living and whose victims rise from the grave to become vampires themselves (interestingly, a human food – garlic – is said to be the best way to keep a vampire at bay; see Chapter Seven for foods which preserve and protect). Werewolves too can generate new werewolves by biting, but not killing, their victim, their mythical lore having expanded in the 20th century through a procession of horror movies to rival that of vampires. Zombies, reanimated corpses brought back to some semblance of life by sorcery in Haitian belief, have undergone a similar metamorphosis in recent years through films and television programmes like *The Walking Dead*, moving from simple creatures of horror to monsters capable, like werewolves and vampires, of creating new zombies by infecting the living.

In some stories, the hero may turn the hunger of the monster on itself, as for example in one of the *Jack the Giant Killer* tales, in which Jack sits down at table to eat with the deadly giant, boasting that he can out-gorge his opponent. While they are eating (porridge, again!), he starts tipping the food into a bag hidden in his shirt, unobserved by the giant. Then he stands up and announces that his stomach is full, but that this does not matter, as he can empty it and start again. He cuts open the bag and lets all the porridge fall out and then starts eating again. Dumbfounded, the giant asks him how he does this, to which Jack boasts that it is something he often does. Not to be outdone, the stupid monster plunges his knife into his own stomach … and drops down dead, leaving Jack the victor.

Finally, some stories feature those who have survived an encounter with a monster that has eaten some part of them, though typically they are monsters themselves. In

Herman Melville's epic whaling novel *Moby Dick*, the manic Captain Ahab has had his leg bitten off by the white whale he relentlessly pursues, which seems to have endangered his sanity. The elegant but villainous pirate Captain Hook in J.M. Barrie's fairytale *Peter Pan* has lost a hand to the crocodile that lives in Neverland and which has become quite harmless to everyone else, as after tasting Hook's flesh, it ignores others because it only wants the rest of him!

CHAPTER SIX

# The Witch's Kitchen

"Boil thou first in the charmed pot.
Double, double, toil and trouble,
Fire burn and cauldron bubble."

– Shakespeare: *Macbeth*.

There is a story, oft repeated in magical circles, about the late Cecil Williamson, who founded the famous Museum of Witchcraft and Magic on the Isle of Man in the 1940s, employing Gerald Gardner, later to become famous as the 'Father of Wicca' as its resident witch. In 1960, Cecil moved the collection to Boscastle in Cornwall, just down the road from me, and lived there almost until his death. He was in the habit of greeting his kitchen white goods (electrical appliances such as his cooker, washing machine and fridge) every morning and chatting to them like old friends, and after his death, these loyal machines refused to work for anyone else!

My own interactions with kitchen appliances tend to be strictly four-letter ones when they refuse to work properly, and I am not suggesting that any witch start an intense relationship with a 100-kilo cube of metal and microcontrollers. But your actual kitchen – arguably the magical centre of your home – is a different matter.

Witches and other magical practitioners have always known that the home is inherently magical: the magical importance of the threshold and the hearth go back way past the beginnings of history and carry a huge wealth of tradition and lore. Your threshold itself holds an innate protective power which is as old as the very first caves and mud huts inhabited by our ancestors. In the classic vampire film, you may have observed that the vampires cannot enter a house unless they have been invited. This is a firm psychic law, which you can reinforce if you ever feel under attack, by hanging protective amulets around the doorway, sprinkling salt across the threshold and hanging old iron items (old keys work really well) and even garlic around the doorway.

This power also resides in the central 'hearth' of your home, though nowadays this may be a cooker, a wood burner or a central heating system, rather than a real fireplace. If you are unsure, think of what you feel is the heart or centre of your home, whether it is the place you cook or the room you might be likely to huddle in if you felt cold. If you are fortunate enough to own an Aga or similar range, this will serve very well and has the added advantage that it has surfaces on which you can place magical artefacts such as crystals, runes or hag-stones. Many modern homes do not have anything resembling a fireplace, but the kitchen can be relied on to fill in for this amenity and be magical of itself, because you spend so much time there, creating and working. This makes perfect sense when you remember that the aforementioned mud hut had no kitchen; meals were cooked over the central fire – for which your cooker now stands in. And I suppose the day will come when even the cooker will vanish from our homes, its place being taken by some conglomeration of air-fryer, microwave, and other technology not yet thought of. Never mind: where there's a witch, there's a way, and witches will always make their kitchens special and magical with their own items.

My own kitchen is delightfully witchy: I am fortunate enough to live in a very old-looking cottage with exposed beams, stone floors, worm-eaten timber lintels over the lattice-paned windows, and roughcast plaster walls … absolute cosmetic nonsense, as the house was built in 1980! … and it is scattered with witchy images and artefacts, from the shiny witch-ball in the window and the Green Man over the door to the little knitted witch on the dresser, cheek-by-jowl with sun-catchers, charms, crystals, and bunches of drying herbs.

Many witches will not feel comfortable revealing their beliefs and practices in this way to the casual visitor, but there is a middle way. Witches have always been good at concealment!

But let us first take a look at making your kitchen into somewhere that you can work on magic as well as meals.

To begin with, you might want to cleanse and bless your kitchen, especially if you have only lately moved into the house. A good smudging with some sage or other protective and cleansing herb is a good start, and you can wash down the cupboards, walls, and floor with a herbal wash that includes some salt (proper sea salt is preferred), while inchanting the room with your own words, imbuing it with magical intent as your centre of operations.

Inchanting involves the speaking of a magical charm over and over again until you feel it has taken effect. The charm would ideally be a very short rhyme you can speak without a piece of paper and can be muttered under your breath or even recited mentally if others are around who might think it strange.

Invite the Goddess into your kitchen. Ask Her to bless your home and your magical work, and light a candle to

Her on a regular basis. If you are able to have a permanent altar in your kitchen, put fresh flowers on there regularly and make a point of speaking to the Goddess (or the God, if you prefer) as you pass the altar every day. This keeps the energies alive and flowing. The altar can be a very small shelf, tucked away in a corner, and unless you are full-on with deity images and symbols, visitors will just see a shelf with a vase of flowers and perhaps a few *objets trouvés* and think nothing of it. You can hang sacred images in your kitchen and arrange things so that no one else knows they are there. If you have a dresser, images can be placed behind the larger plates standing on the shelves, or a picture can hide them: a framed view of the Cotswolds will not arouse any comment, and only you will know there is a Goddess image on the back – which you can turn outwards if you are working alone in the kitchen. She is a Goddess worshipped by witches down the ages, and She will understand why you turn Her to the wall.

Witch bottles and spirit bottles can also be kept in the kitchen, on a very high shelf where they will pass unnoticed, especially if you have storage jars up there, side-by-side with them. A witch bottle is filled with magical items, such as crystals and herbs and maybe slips of paper with a written inchantment, or it can be a protective, banishing bottle filled with sharp pins (rusty ones are fine) and nails, then topped up with your own urine, or a potion made from carefully chosen herbs and sealed well. It can have a particular purpose, such as protection, or to help you with a special problem, like perhaps quitting smoking or discouraging nosy and intrusive neighbours. The spirit house is something different; it is a glass jar, perhaps an ornate crystal one (get into the habit of frequenting charity shops, as this kind of thing can often be bought for a pound or two), partly filled with sweet-smelling herbs, pretty crystals and other pleasant items, then closed with a prayer for a friendly protective spirit to come and inhabit it. Both bottle and house should be placed inconspicuously. Remember to speak to the spirit in the house every day, even if it's just a muttered "good morning", and to dust his bottle regularly.

Old iron items can be kept on the hearth because the energies of iron discourage some entities – perhaps this is why you so often see old rusty antique irons (the kind for pressing laundry) on cottage hearths, where they also look very attractive and charming. Your kitchen probably has enough iron in the cutlery drawer, the pan cupboard, the machines and the various door hinges to work very well, but there is no reason you should not add any antique items you feel would look attractive and add to the general protective shield. On the threshold, most doors have enough iron (or steel) in their construction or as door furniture to have the same effect, but the magic of iron was understood by our forebears, which is probably why you often see an enormous amount of completely unnecessary thick hobnails hammered into those ancient wooden doors on very old buildings.

Many witches will also grow their own vegetables and herbs for food and for magic and ritual; these will be superior in all sorts of ways, dew-fresh, for one thing, and totally seasonal, thus having more nutrition, a far better flavour, and more power for magical work because the witch will have done things like inchanted them and planted the seeds at the correct moon phase. But of course, not everyone has a garden or space enough outside to grow the things they need. However, magical herbs (aren't they all?) can be grown on the windowsill, and very few non-pagans will be able to tell any that are not culinary from the usual thymes, basils and parsleys. Some plants are very handy to grow in the kitchen for reasons other than cooking or even magic: my kitchen windowsill is never without an aloe vera, for example, because it is sovereign for burns. If I catch myself on a hot pan, I quickly snip a bit off one of the thick fleshy leaves and squeeze the cool gel from the inside onto the burn. It soothes the pain instantly and causes the burn to heal much faster. Some herbs, such as basil, repel insects as well as being useful to the cook as ingredients, and of course lavender has always been used, in little sachets hung in the wardrobe, to repel moths and in potpourri to scent rooms.

Now to how you use your kitchen. Entering your kingdom – or queendom – should arouse feelings of pleasure in you (if it doesn't, then maybe you are fated not to be a kitchen witch). The shine of your pans on their hangers, the gleam of the clean sink and worktops, the tidy array of herbs and spices, the glittering promise of the kettle and the background aroma of food and cleaning materials should all contribute to making you feel at home and ready to work. Whether or not you actively address yourself to the Goddess, you should feel attuned to your magical abilities, as well as just your culinary ones.

Witches will work in a certain way when they are preparing food; their training and knowledge make this natural to them. But the interesting thing is that so will most women (apologies to any men reading this who are domestic gods in their own right, but my feeling is that this is something which is inherited through the mitochondrial DNA, through mothers and grandmothers and aunts). Take cake mixing – or mixing any food that requires it to be amalgamated in a large bowl: any woman doing this automatically moves the spoon sunwise, clockwise, as she mixes. This is either because of, or a simple coincidence with, an ancient belief that clockwise motions encourage growth and rising, a desired outcome for bread or cakes, as well as positivity, happiness, healing and good fortune. You may also find that most women automatically clean any surface in an anti-clockwise direction, removing grime in the magical direction for *banishing*, thus discouraging dirt and negative energies.

*"I would fire a cantankerous cook even if I had to live on dog biscuits for the rest of my days, for everything she touches she poisons for a sensitive person,"* remarks Wilfred Maxwell, the somewhat immature hero of Dion Fortune's magical novel *The Sea Priestess*. He is quite right: many people do not realise the effect of the mood and intentions of the person preparing the food on those who eat it. Could this also contribute to the well-known ill effects of too much junk food? No poor student working in a burger joint, overworked and poorly paid, is going to feel much goodwill towards the customers who flock in an unending stream towards the counter clamouring for service. Equally, home-cooked food is esteemed for its wholesomeness, for the care and love that has gone into its preparation. Any caring mother, cooking a meal for her family, puts her own loving intentions into the food – consciously or unconsciously – even as she adds seasoning. She bestows the same care on the food emotionally as she does on the choice, the quality

and freshness of the ingredients, the hygiene with which she handles them and the care with which they are cooked.

In the same way, a witch might put magical intentions into food more proactively, inchanting the food, even including ingredients (hopefully not poisonous ones!) chosen for their magical qualities. What better way to heal a quarrel, for example, than a gift of cupcakes, iced with pink hearts and filled with ingredients chosen to enhance positive feelings like kindness and love?

The kitchen witch – and the Wiccan as well – will use her kitchen for many other purposes than mere cooking, including creating her own herbal potions for magic, making herbal cures and remedies, binding smudge sticks from herbs, making her own candles and incenses, and cleaning her altar tools.

Kitchen-witchery implies a less formal, less structured, less rule-bound way of working magic, involving less in the way of 'magical hygiene' and perhaps more imagination and the giving of free rein to one's creative instincts. Where a coven witch would cast a circle for all magical and ritual work and use tools that have possibly been created for the purpose but certainly cleansed and consecrated and even named, a kitchen witch might reach for an ordinary saucepan instead of an antique cast iron cauldron and a simple wooden spoon, such as are sold by the million in hardware and cookware shops, in place of a hand-carved wand bound with copper and set with crystals. Her circle is her kitchen, and her rules her own, for what can go amiss in her own domain, surrounded as she is by her own protections, both those inherent in her home and those she has created herself? And don't forget that the witches of former times, persecuted by the Christian Church and always seeking safety in secrecy, kept no obvious magical tools. Their athame (witch's magical knife) was a simple kitchen knife from the drawer; the pentacle (altar plate) was a plate from the dresser with symbols drawn on it in charged water; their Cup was a simple cup taken from the dresser.

It is up to you whether you observe the same kind of distinction in your kitchen as you do in your temple and keep magical tools in a separate drawer, using them only for magical work, or whether you use anything that is to hand, with the knowledge that it is yours, after all, and just as special as a pentacle-engraved, consecrated altar tool. Whatever works for you will work for you.

Of course, a witch steps outside her own protected circle when she heads off to the shops, and while this is a necessary operation, it can be stressful and damaging to your spirit and your mood in a lot of ways. We all hate food shopping, and we all assume that it is about the tedium, the queuing and the trolleys with square wheels...but that is only a part of the story. Supermarkets are filled with negative energies because they are also filled with very unhappy people giving off negative vibes, because grocery shopping is boring and tiresome, and also perhaps because they are worried about the money they are spending – this vibe is noticeably worse in times of national financial depression.

However, individuals may easily construct protection for themselves whenever and wherever they feel the need for protection from negative forces around them, by a number of exercises involving visualisation. A witch may, for example, strongly visualise herself donning a suit of silver or white armour and putting on the helmet, or she may mentally place a floor-length veil over her head and body, strongly envisioning this as turning away negative or malign influence. A mental brick wall or a mini circle cast around oneself is also effective, as is the visualisation of a blue pentagram on the forehead with lines of blue light around the body. I use a thick, heavy cloak of dark cloth which I fasten at the throat; it then hangs down to the floor, and I then mentally reach up and pull the thick, heavy hood down over my face, 'concealing' myself completely. With practice, this kind of visualisation is easy to maintain and will protect you just as well as a cast circle. Most witches who use this form of protection regularly have had the experience of a friend or neighbour walking straight past them in the street without noticing them!

The shopping itself may rely on a hastily scribbled list including bread, milk and toilet paper, but you should also allow your intuition to draw you to the foods your body wants ... Your body knows exactly what you need and (astonishingly) where to find it, and if that's junk food, fat and sugar, go with it, as long as it's not every day. When I was pregnant with my first child, I grew alarmed at the number of chocolate bars I was eating, often three or four a day – I just couldn't stop myself or resist the craving. I raised this with the doctor at my next antenatal check-up, and he smiled and gave me iron tablets. The craving disappeared as soon as I had necked the first tablet, but how did my body *know* that chocolate is a good source of iron? I barely knew it myself.

In the same way, you may find yourself drawn to items you do not need for eating but which later prove themselves ideal for a magical working. This witchy intuition has saved me many a trip to the shops for something I need but don't have in stock. Some spices and herbs just give off magical potential in the same way they give off an aroma…no witch can resist them.

Finally, a witch cannot ignore the magic of cooking itself – and I'm not talking about potions here but real meals to be fed to yourself and your family – not a newt's eye in sight. Many witches make a habit of stirring health, good luck and protection into their dishes as they are making them (just as witches who knit, crochet or do dressmaking stitch good vibes into the garments they make), muttering over the pan and making symbols with the spoon. These ideas go back a very long way. Our Christian ancestors would often cut crosses into foods, either to bring luck and protection to the loved ones who were going to eat them, or because the food itself perhaps needed help in some way: crosses were often cut into loaves of bread to give them a little magical push to help them rise.

Bread itself is one of the most magical foods – and easier to make than most people think. Due to its long preparation time, often involving an hour or more of 'proving' or rising, it offers all sorts of opportunities for the witch to attach blessings and spells to it and then bake them into the finished loaf. When a friend moves house, I have often visited with homemade bread, a little paper package of salt, and a bottle of wine. Witches will recognise this as a sort of 'first footing' at a new threshold, and muggles are happy to see it as a nice house-warming gift.

The making of country wine is another process into which magic is easily incorporated, starting with the selection of the ingredients themselves. All trees and herbs (by which I mean non-woody plants generally) have magical meanings and energies, and when they are suitable for wine-making through having a pleasant flavour and being non-toxic, these can be brought into the wine. Our native UK trees and shrubs particularly lend themselves to Ogham magic, as the Ogham include most fruiting and flowering trees. Apple, for example (*Quert*, in the Ogham alphabet), is excellent for love spells, while elder (*Ruis*), the berries of which have always been a traditional ingredient of wines, are used in all sorts of magics, the tree itself being sacred to the Goddess, and sloes from blackthorn (*Straif*) are used in magic for protection and banishing threats.

CHAPTER SEVEN

# The Food Files

"If this be magic, let it be an art lawful as eating."

– Shakespeare: *The Winter's Tale*.

As a young witch, I was shown the magic of the apple: take the fruit in your hand, with your thumb at the stalk end and your fingers at the blossom end, and cut it in half through the middle. The Goddess's own symbol is then revealed, delineated by the pips and their sharp housings. This is in all apples, from tiny wild crabs to gigantic cooking apples. I was duly impressed. But don't *all* fruits and vegetables carry Her mark? If you grow your own produce, even if it's just the obligatory runner beans, some tomatoes and a few herbs, or if you go out foraging for wild food, for mushrooms, herbs, edible greens, blackberries, sloes and nuts, aren't they *special* in some indefinable way? Maybe it's the glamour of the dew on their skins in the quiet garden in the early morning, or your own sense of achievement in growing or finding them or a feeling of being close to nature and close, too, to our forebears, who grew their own everything in their cottage gardens because there were no supermarkets, no online shopping, and no delivery vans.

But the magic of Life – with a capital 'L' – is in all living things, and perhaps plant life hangs onto it for a bit longer than animal tissue does, for a vegetable that has been cut from the main plant goes on living for quite a while longer than the flesh of an animal which has been killed. The seeds hold the promise of renewed life; even the stalks and other tissues of the vegetable can regenerate – as anyone who ever did the clever trick with the top of a pineapple can tell you. Whole plants can regrow from tiny cuttings or from their own roots if they have been cut down. And it goes on … plants that are way past regenerating or reviving into any semblance of life still hold their medicinal and magical powers, even when they have been hung up and dried for months, pulverised and stored in jars in a cupboard.

This is the power that we utilise when we use these materials for magic, and some magical practitioners seem able to pick up anything, a blade of grass or a dead leaf, and make magic with it. Many simple food items, such as a bread roll, an egg or a single apple, can be made the focus of an effective spell which requires little else other than concentration. However, there are edible and potable substances which are seen as innately magical, that almost guarantee the success of anything you do with them, some because they are rare, some because they have weird magical names or strange shapes, some because they are ancient things which have always been meaningful for mankind in terms of survival or hospitality, and some just because they have now entered the catalogue of foods and drinks which are meaningful to people. Some magical things we would not dream of putting between our own lips: the bezoar, for example – a revolting stone-hard clot of hair retrieved from the stomach of an animal, traditionally a goat, and magically prized for its rarity. And of course, there is a large range of fairly poisonous substances which have figured in magical potions down the ages, from mandrake to some of the eye-catching poisonous fungi that grow in our British woods. There are also many things our impoverished ancestors may have eaten, which we would not now consider as food: I once met a man who had eaten rook pie, for example, and Romani people are said to enjoy baked hedgehog, while some foods of poverty still available would not tempt most modern people: tripe, for instance.

But returning to the matter in dish, let us now look at a list – a far from complete one – of basic foods which have magical meaning.

**APPLE:** In modern paganism, the apple is linked to the Second Harvest or Autumn Equinox. Apples ripen towards the end of the summer and particularly around the time of the equinox, on or near to 21st September, and as they are probably the most successfully grown fruit in the UK, they have become very associated with this time, though also with Samhain (Halloween), as apples were traditionally stored for the winter and would have been available in October.

The fruit is loaded with micronutrients, including antioxidants, vitamins such as C and K, fibre, beneficial substances such as pectin, and also water which hydrates the eater. "An apple a day keeps the doctor away," says the proverb, which may be overstating the case, but it is certainly a much healthier choice than many modern snacks for the stomach, the digestion, the heart, the skin, the blood sugar level, the immune system, and the teeth.

The humble apple is found in mythologies, folk tales and customs across the world, from the Ancient Greeks' tale of the golden apples of the Hesperides, which Herakles was instructed to steal as one of his Twelve Labours, to the apple supposedly stolen by Eve in the Bible (actually the Bible does not specify an apple, but rather calls it simply *"the fruit of the Tree of Knowledge"*). The fruit is deeply connected to love Goddesses, such as Aphrodite, who features with her fruit in several tales, including her gift of three golden apples to her protégée, Hippomenes. These he dropped before Atalanta, who paused to pick them up, thus losing a running race with him and being obliged as a result to marry him. Aphrodite also receives the Apple of Discord from Paris, winning the title of most beautiful Goddess from Hera and Athena and kicking off the Trojan Wars. The Romans honoured Pomona, who was a Goddess of fruit generally, but the 'pom' syllable of her name is etymologically related to the word for apple in many European languages. In Norse belief, the Gods themselves were kept young and strong by magical apples, while the apple as a symbol of temptation appears in many a fairy tale and children's story. I could go on all day, but to paraphrase Jeanette Winterson, apples are not the only fruit.

In the ancient Celtic tree alphabet called 'Ogham', the apple tree letter '*Quert*' speaks of love, choices, and health or healing, longevity or even immortality. It can also signify generosity, peace, abundance, and prosperity. The fruit is associated with love and with spells for and about love, notably the simple spell that many young girls would do at Halloween, peeling an apple in one long unbroken strip and throwing this strip over their shoulder to see which letter it formed as it landed: this would be the initial of the man they would marry.

**BANANAS:** Bananas do not seem very magical; in fact they appear to have a rather comical significance in many people's minds, perhaps because of their phallic shape or their association with old-fashioned slapstick comedy.

However, they are useful and magical. As a food, they are healthy, giving you carbohydrates, fibre and vitamins, and also potassium, which can help lower blood pressure. As an interesting aside, their peel makes amazing compost but can also be used to polish shoes!

The bananas you buy for your lunch are a long way removed from the natural banana, being the descendants of a sort which developed without seeds: a natural banana is absolutely stuffed with little seeds which make it more or less inedible. They are technically a berry!

The banana plant (not a tree but a large herb) is protective, and the fruit speaks of fertility and abundance and can be used in love spells (or lust spells, actually, as its shape speaks of sex rather than romance). The yellow colour speaks of success and achievement, so a banana will 'fire up' a spell, and it is associated with the moon because of its shape and colour.

**BEER:** This ancient drink is also favoured as a libation to masculine grain and fertility Gods and may be used in the Cup instead of wine as the ritual draws to a close. The drink is made from grains, which undergo malting (sprouting), boiling and brewing, so it is particularly associated with harvest rites. Hop flowers are generally added to many beers to add flavour and improve their keeping properties. The different kinds of brewed liquors, ale, beer, lager, and stout, all have different meanings in ritual and different uses in magic; for example, stouts for strength and resilience, ales for clarity, and darker beers for grounding. It does not need to be said (though I will say it anyway) that a good beer from a local Indie brewery will be better for magical purposes than a can of something from the supermarket.

**BLACKBERRIES:** In common with other trees and shrubs that bear white blossoms and red or black berries, these are linked to the Otherworld and, in the case of the blackberry, strongly linked to the Fae. In rural France to this day I am told that many older people will not eat these fruit 'à cause des Fées', while in Britain an ancient superstition warns you not to pick them after Michaelmas, as 'the Devil has dragged his tail (or in some versions, cursed them or even urinated) on them.' Unusual to begin with, blackberries bear flowers, unripe fruit and ripe fruit all at the same time and even on the same branches, and the flower – if you examine it closely – has a strong resemblance to a wild rose (they are both members of the Rosaceae family and both have ferocious thorns). The jewel-like fruits are sweet and delicious; good for making desserts and wine; also rich in vitamin C and flavonoids; and a favourite goal for wild food enthusiasts. To the gardener's despair, the blackberry vines have a habit of 'leapfrogging' – throwing out long tendrils which, when they touch the ground, root firmly, creating an arch which is fixed at both ends. This was once considered magical, and ailing babies would be passed under the arch in the hope that they would be made well.

The Ancient Greeks associated them, like the grapevine, with Dionysus. In modern paganism, they are linked to the autumn equinox, which is when the fruit is at its best, and in Britain they 'stand in' for grapevines, which do not occur naturally or generally thrive here.

**BREAD:** Is there any culinary aroma more enticing than that of freshly baked bread?

The 'staff of life' is a food found in thousands of forms across all the cultures of the world and made from various types of flour, water, salt, and usually yeast. Easy to make, delicious, nutritious, filling and cheap, it is no wonder it became so important to mankind from the very earliest times.

The cultivation of wheat and barley began in the so-called 'Fertile Crescent' in the Middle East (roughly across modern-day Cyprus, Egypt, Iran, Iraq, Israel, Jordan, Lebanon, Palestine, Syria, and Turkey), where bread-making began some 11,000–14,000 years ago as the rough processing and cooking of wild grains which were later cultivated. The production of bread was to become of huge importance and could be said to have shaped our civilisations and our settlements around the farmers and bakers who produced it.

"The eating of bread is according to the will of god," said the Ancient Egyptians, who were the first people to use yeast to make softer, risen bread. Leavened bread was a staple from the earliest period of the joined kingdoms of Upper (southern) and Lower (northern) Egypt, c.3,000 BCE, eaten by pharaoh and commoner alike. The grain used was emmer, a relative of modern wheats which is quite hard to process and grind, so many mummies have been found with damage to their joints, probably from the long-term use of a stone quern to grind the grain. This process also caused damage to the teeth of the consumers, and dental abscesses were a common (and very painful) cause of premature death in Ancient Egypt. Although their diet was pretty sugar-free (just some honey and sweet fruits like dates and figs), the grindstone contributed to the content of the bread, and the grit and other inclusions wore down the teeth until the dental pulp was exposed to bacterial decay, leading to abscesses: the lady Pharaoh Hatshepsut was one famous victim of this health condition.

Every culture has its own forms of bread, which are suited to its climate, the accompanying cuisine, the common family habits and the taste of the nation. Bread comes in many shapes across the world: bagels and challah from Israel, baguettes and croissants from France, ciabatta and focaccia from Italy, cornbread from America, lavash and pitta from the Middle East, mantou from China, paratha and naan from India, and pumpernickel from Germany. In some cultures, bread is more than a side dish: it may be the dish itself and the utensil used to eat it – as for example the array of flatbreads that may accompany an Indian curry, such as chapatis, which were originally provided to scoop up the seasoned meat and sauces. In Britain in mediaeval times, the rich would enjoy their meat on a 'trencher', a flat round of bread which was not designed to be eaten – by the rich. It was there to protect the table and the clothes, to catch gravy and crumbs of meat, and afterwards it might be taken to the castle gates and given to the poor.

In Britain, bread has been subjected to some indignities: for example, supermarket white bread, produced with the Chorleywood method and baked so that it has no crust and a texture (and flavour) similar to wallpaper paste. This was what I was brought up on in the 1960s because it was more affordable for families on a budget. As a reaction to this and due to their perceived health benefits, brown and wholemeal breads have gained hugely in popularity – though white bread still outsells brown in the UK.

But bread has never been mere food: from its earliest beginnings, it has gained importance spiritually, politically, and culturally. Wars have been fought over it, riots have been staged and political careers have been built or have foundered on bread. "Give them bread and circuses," advised the Roman poet Juvenal, pointing to the vital importance of this food to the population.

Bread was often an offering to the Gods in many cultures, and to this was added sweet baking: honey cakes and fruited cakes made impressive offerings, guaranteed to please the deities. In many temples past and present, food was eaten as part of the ritual, and bread became a vital part of these traditions. It is cheap to produce, delicious to eat and can be flavoured, shaped, and decorated to suit the occasion.

Every culture has had deities specially connected to bread, such as Demeter and Ceres, the Greek and the corresponding Roman Goddesses of corn; golden-haired Sif, the Norse corn Goddess; the Spartan Deipneus, God of grain and baking; and Isis and Osiris, whose life cycle brought fertility to the land and grain into the jars. The Romans even had a Goddess called Fornax, the Goddess of the bread oven!

I have already mentioned the Christian tradition of the Eucharist, bread eaten as part of religious communion, but other faiths often have their own version of this. In Wicca, we finish the ritual with *Cakes and Wine* (see under Cake), but at Lughnasadh (around 1st August) bread very much comes to the fore as pagans celebrate the First Harvest, which is themed on the production of grain.

Bread as a symbol means life and the sustaining of life, to the extent that 'bread' became a slang word for money in the UK from the 19th century (it may derive from Cockney rhyming slang: bread and honey = money) and from the 1930s in the US.

Spiritually and symbolically, bread speaks of community and fellowship, so that in the past even a bandit might think twice before assaulting, robbing or killing a man with whom he had *broken bread*. In ritual it becomes a sacred sharing of nourishment (though generally some kind of sweet cake is provided rather than plain bread) and a means of helping to ground the participants who may have experienced otherworldly visions and insights or taken part in magic.

**CAKE:** Sitting next to bread on the shelf, cake has deserved a place in this index for its deliciousness but also for its role in human affairs. Got a celebration, a rite of passage, a birthday or an anniversary going on? Cake is the answer, as the saying goes. Feeling down in the dumps and need something to lift your mood? Cake again! One sign of how important it is is that everyone's wedding photographs include at least one shot of the cake. And traditionally, one tier of that cake would be kept, well wrapped and hoarded up, for the christening of the first child, a magical linking if ever I saw one.

Cake is associated with celebration in all languages – *making cake memories*, as one expression describes it – and many sayings show it as the object to be desired or a symbol of that ambition. It means achievement, success, triumph ... even to the point of rubbing another's face in your victory, as in the bride who sends a slice of wedding cake to her disappointed rival. I am reminded of O-Lan in Pearl S. Buck's sweeping Pulitzer Prize-winning novel *The Good Earth*, spending hours preparing special rice cakes when she visits her previous owner to present her firstborn son. The cakes are made and decorated to the highest standard so that she may demonstrate her new status as wife and mother to the slave owner who treated her with contempt.

A popular way of using cake to explain magic to non-magical people is asking them if they have ever performed a magic spell. They of course reply that they have not. The witch then asks, have they ever made a wish and blown out the candles on their birthday cake? Well … yes, comes the answer. Then you have done a spell! replies the witch. Cake lends itself well to simple magical procedures like this one … literally a piece of cake.

As a coven leader, my style of high priestessing is somewhat domestic: my coveners call me, only half-jokingly, ‘mum’, and I delight in serving them suppers after ritual and baking them cakes for any special occasion. As a woman who loves baking, I have often officiated at a handfasting (pagan wedding ceremony) and provided the handfasting cake as well. Part of my job is also to provide cakes for the ‘Cakes and Wine’ ceremony that concludes a ritual, and these are not just plain bread but a kind of shortbread made with carefully chosen magical ingredients, such as salt and spices, and baked to be suitable for the lifestyle choices of the coveners, particularly veganism.

**CHOCOLATE:** Everyone’s favourite naughty treat and everyone’s go-to idea for a gift, chocolate is a magical substance packed with a cocktail of mind-altering chemicals unsuspected by most people who stop off at a filling station or newsagents and pop a bar on top of their purchase … because who can resist it? Aside from the choccy flavour we have all been conditioned to love from a very early age, the sweet is largely composed of fat and sugar, which our ancient brains are programmed to regard as desirable food. As well as several substances related to caffeine which stimulate the mind and body, it includes phenylethylamine and anandamide, chemicals which contribute to the production of substances such as the ‘happy hormone’ dopamine in the brain; this is why we crave chocolate so much when we have a broken heart and possibly why you can buy chocolate that is specially marketed for love play. And for those who joke that chocolate, as a food derived from beans, must be one of your 'five a day' veggies, it's not total nonsense. Chocolate is also packed with flavonoids, antioxidant and anti-inflammatory substances which are very beneficial to health.

The product itself, which is made from the beans of the cacao tree, which have been fermented, dried and processed, can vary in quality, sweetness, milk content, and cocoa content, according to the regional taste, from US chocolate, which can legally have as little as 10% cocoa, to the very best Swiss and Belgian chocolates, which can be 35% or so. In the UK, the average chocolate product contains around 22% and is sweet compared to the richer, darker chocolates found in Europe. In recent years, high-cocoa solids have become a buzzword in chocolate production, and it is now possible to purchase bars containing 70%, 80% or even 100% – the latter must be quite bitter and nasty to most palates, as it contains no milk proteins or sugar, only pure cocoa solids and cocoa butter.

Chocolate is a popular offering to several deities, including the love Goddesses Venus/Aphrodite, Freyja and Erzulie Freda, also Dionysus, and was of course a usual offering to Quetzalcoatl, the Aztec God with whom it was chiefly associated and to whom it was sacred, as he was said to have given the cacao bean to mankind. The Mayan Goddess Ixcacao was associated with it, being actually a Goddess of chocolate! Dark, bitter chocolate would be a suitable offering for several deities, including Underworld Gods like Hades, Arawn, and Baron Samedi.

Like cake, chocolate has become bound up with celebration, but in this case, 'celebration' as in 'festival'. It has become so deeply associated with the Christian festivals of Christmas and Easter that it has almost displaced the foods originally regarded as the seasonal treats that went with them. Plum duff (Christmas pudding)? Once a *sine qua non* for the main meal on 25th December, it is now just one of multiple choices that include chocolate desserts, and you can be sure chocolate makes an appearance after the meal, if not during it. And as for Easter, it isn't anything that came out of a chicken that a child expects on Easter morning! Outside the seasonal events, it has become a byword for indulgence, so that advertising desserts and confections made from chocolate with this term has become a cliché. Another association for chocolate is *reward*. Had a bad day at work? Get a chocolate bar on the way home (that's the dopamine thing). Achieved something you are pleased with yourself about? Treat yourself to choc. Even the dog gets a chocolate if he has been good (special dog chocs, obviously, as real chocolate is poisonous to many animals). There is a feeling of *entitlement* around eating the product which goes back through many decades of family customs and imaginative advertising, including the names of chocolate-based bars, and which makes it a desirable offering to any deity or even the centre of a fun ritual about life's pleasures.

Cacao, the raw plant material from which chocolate is made, is also eaten, though it is very dry to eat, and can be added to a chilli to enhance the flavour. It is also used in spiritual work, sometimes as a drink, but without the milk solids and sugar which commercial chocolates contain. The drink or food is said to promote spiritual awareness and open the mind and spirit to enlightenment, and the ceremonial consumption may be followed by prayer, meditation or some other activity such as dowsing or reading tarot.

**CHERRIES:** Life is a bowl of cherries, they say, and I wish this were true for more people. But these plump red fruits, with their intoxicating hint of almond, are actually super magical. I expect many readers are thinking of that disgusting scene in *The Witches of Eastwick*, but cherries may be used for magic to help and heal and are particularly useful in love spells. Many children of previous generations knew the little divinatory rhyme that goes *"Tinker, tailor, soldier, sailor, rich man, poor man, beggarman, thief."* This was a little counting rhyme used to number the stones left on your plate after eating cherries and would supposedly tell you what you would become (or who you would marry) when you were grown up. Culpeper assigns them to Venus, which you can understand when you look at their shape and colour and flavour, and their red bloom suggests their magical link with health, vitality and energy – like most fruit, they are very good for the health and contain vital micronutrients and flavonoids. Their red colour not only suggests sex but also links them to the base chakra, which is about basic physical needs. People speak of 'losing your cherry' when they mean having your first sexual experience.

Unlike most *Prunus* species, most cherry trees do not have thorns; however, they do contain cyanide – which is what gives them their almondy flavour. This is mainly concentrated in the kernels of the stones, so although a few cracked stones may be left in jam, for example, for extra flavour, it is not wise to eat too many. Cherries are the first trees to bloom in the spring.

**CIDER:** A quintessentially English drink, cider was observed (and even sampled, maybe?) by Julius Caesar when he first arrived in Britain in 55 BCE and saw the Britons making the drink from native crab apples. It must have been quite a bitter drink, having been made from these sour little fruits, and modern ciders are much sweeter. They are made from a variety of apples and in a variety of ways to give sweet, dry, clear, or cloudy ciders, which are also popular across Europe and other countries. While it is a health-giving drink and the consumption of cider vinegar has been linked by some proponents to improved health and weight loss, cider was also historically associated with lead poisoning – *Devon colic* – and resultant blindness, as the vessels used for the drink were made from lead, often deliberately, as the sweetness the dissolved (but toxic) metal gave to the drink was enjoyed.

Because the apple is sacred in modern paganism, so too is the 'wine' made from its juice, which is associated with and used at the three harvest Sabbats of Lughnasadh, Descent, and Samhain, perhaps originally because the apples were ripe in the late summer, so the cider-making would commence then. Cider is a good choice for libations to any fertility deity or any deity of love, particularly when sweetened with honey.

Because it is associated with love and with love deities, it has been used for simple country magic and divination, such as the Halloween apple peel trick described in Chapter Three.

**COFFEE:** Coffee is magic in itself, if you ask me. Anything that can get me out of bed in the morning with my eyes actually open and ready for work is a miracle in itself. The drink (and in magic, you should use proper coffee beans – instant just won't do) brings energy to any spell and is also a favoured libation for chthonic and death Gods like Baron Samedi and also Gods associated with energy, thunder, and storm, like Thor and Zeus. In the Middle East, where it is even more important in everyday life than it is in the UK, it is used by the Sufis to induce an ecstatic state.

**EGGS:** A symbol of new beginnings, rebirth and spring, as well as a very complete food packed with protein and micronutrients, eggs have long been a focus of magical practice. A single egg can be used as the focus for a simple spell, or coloured and decorated for a festival. It can be used magically as a sort of poppet, perhaps drawn or painted with the likeness of a person and with some of their hair glued on before being treated magically as the person in question in the spell. If you find this hard to believe, remember that the children of World War II were encouraged to draw a rough facsimile of Adolf Hitler's face, with the cowlick hair and the toothbrush moustache, on their breakfast egg – and then smash it in with their spoons! Even the shells, well washed and ground to powder, can be used almost like salt in protection spells. I have found no mention anywhere of what kind of eggs should be used, but I feel it makes sense to use fertilised free-range eggs for important magic, rather than the infertile battery eggs commonly available in supermarkets (though many shops have now adopted the policy of selling only 'happy' eggs from free-range chickens). Eggs are often used in spellwork to improve one's finances and for spells for general good fortune. Duck eggs might also be suitable for magic, particularly that involving emotions (associated through magical correspondences with the element of water), and they even have blue-tinted shells.

Pagans link the egg to the spring equinox (Ostara), just as Christians associate it with their spring festival of Easter.

**FIGS:** The symbolism associated with this plant is a strange mix: it is strongly associated with sex, particularly female sexuality, and few people in a Christian culture will hear the words 'fig leaf' without thinking of Adam and Eve in the Garden of Eden. Yet it is also linked with spiritual wisdom and development, with traditions such as Buddha achieving enlightenment while meditating under a Bodhi, or sacred fig tree.

Figs are used in love and sex spells and for protection, fertility and knowledge.

**FLOWERS:** Yes, flowers! You probably eat more of these than you realise. Some foods are made from or flavoured with flowers, for example, Turkish delight and rose harissa seasoning, which both contain extract of roses; cloves, which are buds of a member of the myrtle family; and marigolds, which have traditionally been used to flavour soups and stews. Other flowers are simply eaten because they are delicious, including artichokes, which are the buds of the globe artichoke plant *Cynara cardunculus*, or courgette blossoms, wonderful stuffed, dipped in batter and fried. Many herb flowers are eaten because they are part of the plant or deliberately because they look pretty and taste nice in salads: nasturtiums, mint, chives, and borage, for example, or in baked goods, such as sweet cakes and muffins. Banana blossoms came into vogue a few years ago as a vegan substitute for fish; sold in cans, they have the texture of white fish and are flavoured with seaweed.

But edible flowers really come into their own when they are introduced to egg white and sugar and become crystallised flowers, which have a range of uses in patisserie or can just be eaten like sweets. Very colourful flowers or petals, like rose, pansy and violet, are the most suitable, and of course care must be taken not to choose flowers which are toxic in any way.

Magic? Well, what would you think, given that these plant components are so deeply associated with courtship and love? Flowers have other associations as well, though, including healing quarrels, wishing someone well who is ill, remembering the beloved dead, and celebrating special occasions. As plants have their own tables of correspondences, this would be your guide on which flowers to use in your magic; for example, roses: love, always love! They have a further level of correspondences attached to their colours, so pink roses for love and red ones for passion. Yellow flowers are sunny and speak of good fortune and hope, while blue ones mean healing, and if you really want to take the subject further, there is a language of flowers, with each one having an established meaning.

**GARLIC:** Setting aside the associations with vampire lore, garlic has always been seen as a magically purifying and protective plant (strangely, as one of its better recognised effects on the human body is to give one foul breath and smelly perspiration!). Yet our forebears were wiser than we knew: garlic is so purifying that it can be used in place of antibiotics and antivirals. It purifies the blood and helps the heart stay healthy. It will see off a cold, and many people swallow garlic capsules every day to protect themselves against colds and flu bugs. It lowers cholesterol levels, and the garlic-derived drug *Allopurinol* is used against gout, which is a condition associated with high cholesterol. It has even been said to act as an insect repellent when taken orally.

Magically, it is used primarily for protection, as well as for purification and spells for healing. The whole bulbs in their papery skin can be strung over doorways and windows to repel negativity and ill fortune or even carried (suitably well wrapped!) in your pocket or handbag to keep you from harm. The individual cloves can be used in spells to drive away negativity or banish things or people; they are easy to write on with a pin or knife tip (the letters become visible as they turn brown with oxidation as the flesh is exposed to the air) to imbue them with intent. Strangely, it can also be used in love spells, but a spell using garlic to banish an unwanted admirer might be very effective (or you could just get into the habit of eating garlic and breathing it at him!).

**GRAPES:** Sacred to many fertility deities, such as Dionysus and Bacchus, black and white grapes are a symbol of wealth, generosity and hospitality, as well as fertility and harvest. Their cultivation goes back around 8,000 years in the Middle East, where they originate and where the earliest wines were produced in Georgia on the shores of the Black Sea, later spreading to Ancient Egypt, Greece, and around the Fertile Crescent.

Wine production has spread across the world into the Americas, Australia and New Zealand and even into Britain. Its use in religious ritual has been well established, probably for as long as it has been around. Both grapes and wine are highly suitable for libation, and in magic for fertility and prosperity.

**HERBS:** Herbs are famously magical, even the culinary ones (thyme is as magical as deadly nightshade and considerably more so than so-called enchanter's nightshade), but they deserve a book of their own, so I will do no more than list a few common green culinary and garden herbs and what they are for, as examples. **Basil** is one of those herbs that seems to have a place in every kind of work. It is protective, cleansing, healing, connected with love, psychic and spiritual work of all kinds ... and delicious on pasta! **Bay** was the Roman laurel, connected with the sun and also strongly with the idea of success and victory, so it will bring success into any working you do. It was also the material that was burnt under the tripod of the Sybils, oracular priestesses who worked at Delphi and other sites and went into trance because of the fumes from the burning bay leaves (don't try this at home), so it is associated with divination and divine messages. A bay tree is a lovely thing to have in your garden: it is handsome, evergreen, and protective, as well as useful, but be careful, as it will get very big. Bay leaves not only go into soups and stews but can also be used to write your magical intent on for a spell and then burnt to release the power. **Lavender**'s name comes from the Latin word for washing, as its powerful scent is lovely on freshly laundered clothes. I often put a few drops of the essential oil into the washing machine if I have some particularly smelly clothes to clean. It has a thousand uses in magic and also in the kitchen (lavender cakes, scones and muffins have enjoyed a recent vogue); the laundry; for beauty; and the medicine box: try rubbing it into a strain, sprain or bruise (it is the only essential oil recommended for applying undiluted to the skin). **Lemon balm**, which is very easy to grow in the garden and makes delicious lemony tea, is used in spells for improved health and long life, as well as being very useful for relieving stress. **Mint** is a very useful cleanser – its robust scent and taste (which is used to flavour most toothpastes) have led to its being used to refresh and cleanse all kinds of things, and not only one's breath. Add it to washes to cleanse and consecrate magical tools or to re-consecrate items that have been touched by another without your permission, or add it to an herbal bath if you are about to receive initiation. As a healing herb, it will help sort out indigestion and trapped wind. **Parsley** has a reputation for being hard to grow, but it can be bought in your local supermarket in bundles or in pots. It is an incredibly healthy thing to eat, as it is packed with iron, calcium, and vitamin C, with many other micronutrients, and it is also a natural breath freshener that will defeat even garlic and is said to purify the blood. It is associated with love and lust, fertility, and prosperity but also helps with psychic work. **Rosemary**, like its relative lavender, is about purifying and cleansing but also helps with mental powers and memory. **Sage** is well-known for its cleansing and banishing properties, and many practitioners will routinely cleanse a space by wafting around smoke from a smouldering bundle of sage before starting a ritual or even do this in a haunted house to calm down the psychic activity. This is called 'smudging', and in fact most herbs can be used for smudging for different purposes. **Thyme** is another herb that has multiple uses. It is used for cleansing, purifying, protection, love spells, and also a nice cottage pie.

**HONEY:** All foods are magical, and yet how many compare with honey? Stolen from the flowers by bees, digested and processed within the hive, and stolen from them in turn by people prepared to brave the stings, I have heard it said there are substances in honey that defy analysis. I'm not sure I believe that in this day and age, but it is an index of how special, how mysterious, and how magical this food is. It is also a food that many might prefer not to examine too closely: some of the nectar that goes into its production comes from other insects, typically aphids, and of course it is swallowed by the bee and then regurgitated when it returns to the hive. But the true magic of this astonishingly sweet food lies in its ability to heal. Microorganisms cannot live in honey, so it will never go *bad*, though it may turn crystalline and sugary with age. This quality means honey can be used like an antibiotic. Got an infected finger or a burned hand? Try smearing it with honey and covering it with gauze for a day (always consult a doctor if symptoms persist). It can be taken by mouth for coughs and colds (see under Spices further down this chapter for the recipe) and used as a facial mask to improve your skin. A few years ago, Manuka honey was hitting the headlines for its health benefits, but all honeys have benefits, and as a food, it is both delicious and good for you – unless you are diabetic. Although, in fact, honey is better for the health of even diabetics than sugar, as it has many micronutrients and a lower glycaemic index, meaning it does not cause the body to produce so much insulin.

The magic of honey also applies to its producers, and beekeepers have all kinds of interesting beliefs about their hives and bees, including the traditional belief in 'telling the bees' – that the bees must be told of any family changes, such as a death, birth or marriage, or they will desert the hive and fly away, or even die.

Honey has almost universally been used as a metaphor for the sweetness of life, of a situation, or of a person and has been used as an offering to the Gods in rituals of gratitude, particularly after harvests. Honey is often added to libations, liquid offerings poured out for the Gods both in antiquity and by modern pagans. In the Bible, it was associated with the Promised Land and with good eating generally (locusts and honey: a revolting idea to modern Western ears!). In Greece, Apollo and Artemis were associated with bees and were thus offered honey, and the sacred *Deipnon* suppers offered to Hecate at the crossroads would often include it. In Ancient Egypt, it was offered to the Nile and to fertility and pleasure deities like Hat-Hor and Bast. Ancient Egyptian families might put some in a dish in the home shrine for their ancestors or for Bes, the little God who protected the home and families. In Hinduism, honey is one of five ingredients (along with milk, yoghurt, ghee, and sugar) which make up the magical elixir *Panchamrit*, sometimes with spices and fruits added. This is offered to the Gods and also shared as a healing food in the communal meal in the temple.

See also: Mead.

**LEMONS:** Strangely for such a sunny yellow fruit, lemons are associated with and sacred to the moon and are used, with their zests and their essential oil, if any lunar correspondences are needed for a ritual or a spell. Lemons have been associated for a long time with cold cures, perhaps because they contain a fair bit of vitamin C and also antioxidants, but chiefly, I believe, because the lemon drink, especially if sweetened with sugar or honey, is soothing for a dry, sore throat; its sharpness cuts through that awful gluey feeling that fills your mouth and throat when you are unwell. Lemons are also cleansing and purifying, both physically and magically.

Their colour links them with the solar plexus chakra, which is about confidence and personal power but also the centre of stress and emotion (as in when you are nervous about something and get that 'butterflies' feeling).

**MEAD:** A wine brewed from honey, sometimes with herbs and other flavourings added, this delicious and magical drink has gained huge popularity with modern pagans, as it did with its original creators, probably in Africa, though we have come to associate it primarily with the Norsemen and the Celts. For its sweetness, it has become associated with love and marriage, and it is a usual drink at pagan handfastings and often at the Beltane celebrations as both a communal drink and a libation to the Gods. The very term 'honeymoon' is said to be a reference to the sweetness of the first few days of marriage, as opposed, cynically, to those which follow. Some traditions aver that there was an ancient custom of drinking mead for the first 30 days of the marriage – which must have led to some fearsome hangovers in that period!

Pagans use mead as a popular libation at harvest Sabbats as well as at Beltane and any celebration of a wedding or anniversary: my own Golden Wedding anniversary included a drinking horn of mead provided by my wonderful high priest, who wrote and officiated at a special handfasting for my husband and myself to celebrate our 50 years of marriage.

**MEAT:** Many magical practitioners will not use meat in their magic or ritual because it necessarily involves the death of an animal, but in some pagan streams, such as Voodoo, blood sacrifice is still practised and meat is a regular component, whether as a sacrifice or as the focus of magic. I have known animal products used in witchcraft in this country; for example, a young witch I know recently used a whole cow's tongue to stop nasty gossip that was being spread about a friend. Magical dinners may be prepared for a date as part of a love spell – or for a spell to end a relationship – and the meats (including fish and shellfish) would be carefully chosen to this end. Meat may be used as a poppet, an effigy of a person which is treated as you wish the person to be treated – stuck with pins or wrapped in rose petals, according to how you feel about them. Bones and other animal parts may also form the focus of a spell, in the same way that herbs and other items can be used. However, care should be taken not to kill an animal just for one spell, and the animal should be honoured beforehand.

**MILK AND DAIRY:** The magic of the dairy does not stop with the arrival of fresh foaming milk from the cow. For thousands of years, people have not only drunk milk but transformed it into wonderful and nourishing foods by processes whose discovery must have been some kind of miracle. Fresh full cream milk is churned, agitated for a long time in a clean vessel until lumps of butter form, and can be taken out, rinsed, salted and used or kept. The remaining liquid, which is buttermilk, also has culinary uses, and today is often added to margarines to give them that authentic dairy flavour. Milk can also be warmed and split into curds and whey with rennet, an enzyme from a calf's stomach – although most cheese manufacturers today use an artificial rennet – the basic procedure for cheese making. The cream from the top of the milk, skimmed off with a special flat perforated spoon, or today by machine, has a thousand uses in the kitchen and the patisserie, while in the west of England cream has been gently heated and skimmed to make *clotted cream* for many generations, and a Swiftean but good-natured war still continues between the people of Cornwall and Devon as to whether the jam or the cream goes on the scone first when eating a cream tea!

Dairy products are a symbol of agricultural success, fertility, and wealth, with the word 'cream' having all sorts of connotations of status, ability, and achievement in everyday conversation. "The cat that got the cream," we say of anyone who achieved a greatly desired success, "la crème de la crème" refers to anyone who is at the top of the tree, and "the cream in your coffee" means the thing which brings sunshine into your life. Butter is a symbol of richness and also of enabling: it will grease the way, smooth the path. Ghee (clarified butter) is hugely important in Indian cuisine and has spiritual uses in Hinduism. Milk and milk products are also associated with the pagan festival of Imbolc at the beginning of February, when our ancient ancestors saw the beginning of the longed-for spring in the birthing of lambs and the consequent availability of fresh milk. It may be served, sweetened with honey, in the Imbolc Cup and sent around the circle in place of the more usual wine.

If you use a familiar, whether or not it is in the form of a cat, cream is an appropriate and acceptable offering to pour into its offering bowl after it has worked for you.

**NUTS:** These are associated through many mythologies and folktales with knowledge, messages, and secrets learned. Probably the best-known legend concerns the *Salmon of Knowledge* in Celtic belief. This ancient fish owed its legendary sagacity to its diet of hazelnuts, which grew on nearby trees and fell into the Well of Wisdom, where they formed a regular snack for the salmon. In a related tale, young Fionn Mac Cumhaill became the wisest of the wise, possessing all worldly knowledge, after he accidentally tasted the fish's flesh in a tale very similar to that of Ceridwen and Taliesin. Being left in charge of cooking the salmon for his master, who had spent years seeking it out for its magical gift, Fionn burnt his hand on the salmon as it cooked, put his hand in his mouth – as you would – and inadvertently stole the gift of knowledge from his master. Unlike Ceridwen, who sought to kill the boy who had hijacked her spell, the master, Finn Eces, took the blow philosophically. Folklore is also full of magical nuts that contain treasures and messages in place of a kernel, particularly hazel nuts (also called cob nuts and filberts), which are the most commonly gathered nuts native to the UK, found in almost every hedgerow. Walnuts, which do look for all the world like little brains when they are shelled, are associated with intellect and thinking. Nuts are associated with male energies and the God and are a suitable libation for Him, as well as being useful in protective charms and charms to help keep a secret.

**ORANGES:** Whereas lemons are associated with the moon, despite being a sunny colour, oranges are now associated in the British mind with Christmas and Yule, so that a whiff of orange scent only needs a soupçon of cinnamon to make you expect to hear sleigh bells.

What may come as a surprise is that the orange is not a natural fruit but a cross between a mandarin and a monster grapefruit-like fruit called a 'pomelo'. Also, its vibrant colour may not be natural: the fruits often have green patches on them naturally but are treated with ethylene gas, which turns them uniformly orange.

Oranges quickly became popular with the rich, who could afford to grow the trees in orangeries and did so from the 17th century as a status symbol, as well as a delicious and refreshing food. The poor tended to get their hands on oranges only in the winter … so arose the tradition of putting an orange into a child's Christmas stocking as a rare and exotic treat, which has led to their being inextricably associated with this time of year, despite being available all year round in today's shops.

In magic, these fruits are associated with the sun and all solar correspondences, such as the Zodiac sign Leo, but also with Yule, the winter solstice, which is celebrated by pagans as the sun's rebirth. The fruit's colour links it to the sacral chakra, the one situated around the level of the womb in a woman, and in both sexes it is linked to sexuality and creativity. And dare I suggest that its colour also links it to Mercurial correspondences so that it becomes of use in magic for communication, learning, wisdom, and the acquisition of knowledge?

**POMEGRANATES:** This fruit has always struck me as being a feast for the eyes, rather than the palate. It is golden, blushing, and gorgeous and even structural, with its perfect globe and stiff blossom-end protrusion, a common heraldic emblem, and a splash of colour in a salad or other dish, while its juice is made into grenadine, a highly coloured, sweet but slightly insipid syrup used in cocktails. However, as a food, the pomegranate is somewhat disappointing: difficult to retrieve from the shell, messy and packed with pith and tough, bitter pips.

Magically, the fruit is a symbol of protection from illness but also of riches, gold, fertility, longevity, and eternal life, though interestingly, in Greek belief, it was also associated with death. Persephone, captured by Hades and carried off to the Underworld, happened to eat six pomegranate seeds while there and so was not allowed to return to the earth. In Christian symbolism, the fruit is often associated with the passion of Christ, possibly because of the resemblance of its juice to blood. The juice can also be used in spells which call for blood.

**PUMPKINS:** The big orange pumpkins that we cut scary faces into and leave around at Halloween are from the US but have had a huge influence on the UK as well, so that we cannot now envisage this pagan festival without seeing pumpkins. Their colour has entered the 'livery' of Halloween and even Samhain, sitting side-by-side with black. Despite this, they are a sun symbol and speak of luck and prosperity, possibly because of the gigantic size they are capable of achieving – in the right conditions, as big as an armchair. Their major role in the fairytale *Cinderella* has associated them with magical changes – but temporary ones, with the change being liable to revert at an inconvenient moment. The scary faces they inherited from their more traditional British forebears, turnips and swedes, which were carved in this fashion to see off bad spirits, but the pumpkins do it better, being larger and much, much easier to carve. The seeds, which are delicious raw or toasted, are very protective, and a semicircle of them in front of your front door might pass unnoticed by the neighbours but will keep negativity at bay, as will a small bag of them in your pocket or bag. Shelled, toasted, and salted, they make a great offering and also a snack for attendees and can also be baked with honey or sugar to make a really delicious treat.

All gourds, including the humble cucumber, can be used in writing magic, the inchantment or intention being scribed into the skin of the developing fruit. As the gourd grows, the writing stretches with the gourd – which can then be used as a central focus of the spell and afterwards as a libation.

**SALT:** Salt has always held magical and spiritual meaning as a substance that cleanses and purifies, probably because from earliest times people have used it for preserving meat and other foods and also because of its flavour-enhancing virtue, both of which must have seemed magical to our forebears. In cultures across the world, it has been used in magical rituals to dispel negativity or evil spirits and to cleanse homes and sacred spaces. Even in Christianity it may be added to the water in baptisms, and superstitious people will throw a pinch of spilled salt over their left shoulder, probably without the slightest idea why they do this. In ancient belief, an angel might sit on the right shoulder to counsel good behaviour, while a devil would sit on the left and whisper temptations. Throwing salt in his face would effectively silence him!

Magical practitioners will use salt in many ways for protection and banishing negativity, including laying down lines of salt across doorways and windows, sprinkling it around a space where there is ghostly or negative activity and including it in potions to bless and protect. Of course, we now have a range of gourmet salts available to us, from simple onion, celery, and garlic salts to Himalayan pink salt, and many witches make *black salt* using ingredients like soot, ground charcoal, eggshells, and even graveyard dirt.

In modern paganism, salt is related to the element of Earth and is placed on the right-hand side of the altar (see Water, below).

**SPICES:** Like herbs, these are a very convenient component of many magical workings, not least because they are probably right there in your food cupboard in an easy-to-use form, ready powdered or in small shapes, such as seeds and pods. Many spices have become connected with happiness, success, and achievement over the centuries, largely, I suspect, because they were once expensive items used only on very special occasions. The well-off housewife would keep them squirrelled away in a locked spice cabinet, the key to which hung about her waist – one old farmhouse near Fowey in south Cornwall is listed purely because it has a surviving spice cupboard next to the fireplace, where the precious spices would have been kept dry. Here are just a few of the more familiar ones, spices you are more likely to have in your pantry: **allspice, anise, cinnamon, cardamom, caraway, coriander, cumin, chilli, cloves, ginger, mustard, nutmeg, paprika, pepper, turmeric, vanilla**. The sweet spices with no heat, such as cinnamon, anise, nutmeg, and cardamom, are used for spells for prosperity: a very simple example is to dust your shoes (lightly!) with cinnamon before attending a job interview. You can also blow cinnamon in through your front door on the first day of the month to bring prosperity. A single nutmeg carried in your pocket can act as a money magnet or can protect the home if placed inside somewhere (in the hearth or by the door). When I am baking mooncakes for my coven at Esbat, I always add some sweet prosperity spices, usually cinnamon, to the dough, not only to flavour them but also to bring luck to those who share them. Little packets of sweet spices with other components such as crystals, herbs, and written spells can be carried in your bag or pocket for general good luck. Vanilla is used primarily in love spells; like all orchids, it is associated with sex. The hotter spices such as chilli and pepper tend to be ruled by Mars and are used in more aggressive magic, such as a spell to chase someone away or even cause them harm. Turmeric … oh lovely golden turmeric … will bring sunshine and healing into your life.

Most spices have healing properties, and members of the ginger family – ginger, turmeric, cardamom, and galangal – are strongly antiviral. A young witch called Sahara once taught me her ginger tea cold remedy, which will see off a cold before it can get established: grate and boil an inch of fresh ginger in water for ten minutes, then add honey and a squeeze of lemon. Pop it in a flask and sip it hot through the day. Cinnamon regulates blood sugar and improves insulin sensitivity, and its flavour means you add less sugar anyway, which is a win-win if you are diabetic. Anise and caraway are a useful go-to if you suffer from indigestion or trapped wind. Cloves are a well-known remedy for toothache because they contain a natural anti-inflammatory and painkiller, as well as being antibacterial. Most spices contain antioxidants, and many are also anti-inflammatory.

**SUGAR:** This food is relatively new in the timeline of food, yet it has been with us for many centuries and has found popularity with magical practitioners for its sweetness, which makes it a pleasant addition to ritual foods and drinks, including libations. Its meaning is just that: 'sweetness', and it is used in spells for love, happiness and prosperity. Yet it has associations which make many witches shun it: not only because it is bad for your teeth and your waistline but also because of its part in the slave trade. Although sugar was made from sugar beet in the East as early as the first millennium, it was not produced industrially from beet until the beginning of the 19th century, and in the meantime, sugar cane had become – and remains – a huge industry. Many fortunes were built on the suffering of others as this commodity was farmed, harvested, and processed by slaves and exported from the Americas.

**TEA:** The term 'tea' can refer to any tisane made by pouring boiling water over herbal material, but is generally recognised as being a drink made in this way from the harvested tip leaves of the *Camellia sinensis* shrub, which have been dried, chopped, and processed. Tea is drunk green, using leaves that have been merely dried, or black, which comes from leaves that have been fermented fully so that they turn dark brown. Now famously the national drink in the UK, where we commonly drink it with milk added, it did not gain general popularity here until the 1700s, as it was very expensive, and rich housewives kept it in a locked caddy and brought it out only for treats and favoured guests.

Tea has some claim to being a health drink, as it is packed with antioxidants and is believed to promote heart health, lower blood pressure and reduce cholesterol.

It has uses in a magical life, most famously as the medium for tea leaf reading, but also for ritual and libation. In Japan, it is the centre of the renowned Tea Ceremony, a ritual carried out by trained Geisha and involving a set of traditional movements which promote spirituality, tranquillity, and harmony.

**WATER:** Yes, it is a material that we drink, and it is necessary to our bodies, for life. The saying goes that you can live three weeks without food, but only three days without water, from which, of course, we are largely composed. We need it for digestion, respiration, cooling with perspiration, eliminating waste, and many other functions.

Water has been a regular offering to pagan Gods, now and in the past, and it is also the physical representation of the Element Kingdom of Water, which most modern pagans place in the West. Pagan altars will typically include a bowl of water on the left-hand or west side, and in most witchcraft traditions the water plays a vital role in purifying and consecrating the sacred space before ritual (as well as having been used by the attendees beforehand as they bathe or shower to ritually cleanse themselves ahead of the working). In Wicca, the high priestess will bless and consecrate the bowl of water on the altar, then hold it up for the high priest, who blesses the salt and then stirs it into the water. This is then used in the casting of the circle, being sprinkled around the perimeter (and even on to the coven members). Water is used in some initiations – just as it is used in Christian baptism.

Tap water or rainwater, or even water drawn from someone's well, may be used in ritual, but water gains a whole new magical dimension when it flows to the surface at a sacred well or spring. Pagans will make pilgrimages to the holy springs in Glastonbury or one of the many holy wells in Cornwall and other places and collect the water to take home for special ritual and magical work. Dew, gathered from the grass in the early morning, may also be magical: many women I know make a point of bathing their faces in this moisture on the morning of May Day, as it is believed to enhance beauty. Sea water, while not potable, can also be magical through its associations with the marine deities, and *water from the ninth wave* is an ingredient in some magical work. Deciding which is the ninth wave is, of course, problematic, but a true witch will use his or her instinct and let the sea speak to them with perhaps a minuscule pause in the waves to indicate that a cycle of nine is beginning. Finally, water may be rendered even more magical as *moon water,* water which has been left out in a bowl (ideally made from silver or crystal) to be imbued with the energies of the full moon: I will not go into any further detail, as this subject is covered quite comprehensively in my book *Moontides* (2025), published by Green Magic.

Water is the element of emotion in pagan belief, ruling love and friendship, inspiration and imagination, sorrow, courage, dreams, travel, and partings and used by magical practitioners in magic around all these things. It also represents cleansing and purification, and when it occurs in large bodies, such as deep lakes and seas, it speaks of mysteries and even fear.

Pagans will not only cleanse themselves specially for rituals and certainly for initiations and inductions into a magical group such as a coven, but will also use special substances for bathing prior to initiations, perhaps using sea salt and magical herbs in the bath or tied in a cloth in the shower. Water is also used for magical banishings and rebirthing rituals.

**ICE:** In some cases, frozen water can be used in ritual, perhaps as it melts, to represent something being released or reawakened, or a freezer spell might be used, with a poppet and other items representing him or her being packed up with due ceremony and placed in the deep freeze to bind a troublesome person from doing harm.

**VINEGAR:** This is a step beyond wine, in that it is wine transmuted into yet another product by a fermentation-like process involving a vinegar 'mother'. This is a bacterial substance which has the power of turning wine, or beer, into vinegar, and country winemakers are always adjured not to let the wine 'even *see* any vinegar' when they are making it, lest the wine be turned before it is even bottled. Vinegar has a number of powers and uses around the kitchen – I have always, for example, made my own kitchen cleaning products by mixing white vinegar with water and a squirt of dish detergent; it smells nice, works just as well as commercially sold kitchen sprays and costs a lot less. Like salt, it has been used from earliest times as a preservative, though foods treated with it become *tracklements* rather than mainline food, as soaking in vinegar makes the substance difficult to digest in large quantities, as well as being an acquired taste.

Vinegar is naturally antibacterial: during the Plague, doctors and midwives, who had to go among the infected, soaked their clothing in vinegar, which did in fact offer them some protection, if only from the rat fleas that carried the disease.

In magic also vinegar is cleansing and protecting and is useful in witch bottles, sour jars (a folk magic method of causing problems for an enemy) and in banishings.

**WINE:** *"And much as wine has played the infidel; and robbed me of my robe of honour, well; I often wonder what the vintners buy; one half so precious as the goods they sell."* (Edward Fitzgerald's translation of *The Rubaiyat of Omar Khayyam*).

It is true that wine – in common with all alcoholic drinks – is a double-edged sword, but its place in magic and ritual in almost all traditions is assured. For it is magical: until modern science discovered what yeast could do, no one really understood the magic that turned crushed fruit or juice into this intoxicating, cheering beverage. This process itself links wine symbolically to transformation, as well as to altered mind states associated with spiritual inspiration and mystical experiences.

Wine is almost inextricably associated with parties! Wherever there is a gathering of friends, family or even workmates to celebrate or just to socialise, wine will almost certainly be on the table (except at AA meetings, no doubt), and some wines have become synonymous with celebration in the same way as cake, particularly effervescent wines such as champagne and prosecco. In poetry, wine has become a metaphor for life's sweetness and may be mentioned in connection with the colour of a lover's lips or the sweet taste of her kiss.

In 21st-century Britain, we tend to regard wine with a certain amount of caution: most of us know someone who 'has a drink problem', as we euphemistically call it, or does not know how to stop drinking once they have started and perhaps become silly or even aggressive under the influence. One of the first questions on any medical questionnaire is usually how many units of alcohol you consume on average in a week. We are very aware of its dangers, aren't we? However, these must be balanced against its pleasures as well as its magical uses. From the earliest times, wine was seen as an appropriate offering to the Gods or to the honoured dead. The 'toast', often raised at funeral wakes or otherwise in memory of those who have passed on, has a long history. It is called a toast because of the 17th-century custom of placing toasted bread sprinkled with spices in the glass to flavour the wine. Many spiritualities have a communion or communion-style part, usually towards the end of the ritual. In Neopaganism, this is usually the *Cakes and Ale* or *Cakes and Wine*, a small ritual in which bread or cake and wine are blessed by the high priestess and sent around the circle, with traditional words such as "May you never hunger" and "May you never thirst". In my own coven, this is done with a kiss or a hug, and a careful use of every person's magical name. The custom is a celebration, a bonding ceremony and a means of grounding people who have been experiencing altered spiritual and mental states.

Red wine may also stand in for blood in some rituals and magical practices. In my own coven, we honour this relationship by raising our cups at the end of the ritual and toasting "The blood of the Goddess!" before we open the circle. White wine may be used in some rituals, notably those connected with spring and maiden Goddesses.

The use of wine in magic and ritual can be taken one step further if you decide to make your own **country wines**, as made by generations of country folk through the centuries. Even in chilly Britain, we have a parade of seasonal fruits growing in the hedgerow which are very suitable for wine-making, from blackberries and elderberries through to crab apples and sloes (take care that you know exactly what you are picking, as there are also very poisonous berries often growing side by side with them). The *correspondences* of these fruits can then be woven into the magic or ritual you are doing; for example, sloes are ruled by Mars, so sloe wine (or sloe gin) might be appropriate for a ritual to conjure more physical energy.

CHAPTER EIGHT

# The Food of Festival

"Food to a large extent is what holds a society together, and eating is closely linked to deep spiritual experiences."

– Peter Farb.

As you probably know, pagans celebrate eight festivals, or *Sabbats*, spaced quite evenly around 'the Wheel of the Year', each one different and with a different theme. Some are for new beginnings, some for gratitude, some for remembrance, and some for looking ahead. And each one has its traditional ways of celebrating with food and even its traditional recipes.

Most pagan get-togethers end with the sharing of food. This begins with the simple 'Cakes and Wine', which is a sort of communion at the end of the ritual before the circle is opened, but will often go on to more general feasting, whether that is a set meal at the high priestess's table with napkins and silverware, or bags of crisps and boxes of homemade traybake brought by attendees, or coffee and croissants at the nearby hotel. Catering for pagans at rituals presents a whole new set of challenges for any cook. Not only should the food be appropriate for the festival or other occasion, but it should take into account what is seasonal: many pagans have ethical issues around buying food that has been jetted in from Peru because it is totally out of season in the UK. There is also the fact that many pagans are vegetarian or even vegan. Increasingly nowadays there may also be people there with health conditions like coeliac disease, IBS, lactose intolerance and allergies which mean they cannot eat certain foods. The venue and occasion must also be considered: food may be served in the high priestess's home with her cutlery and plates and seats for all and can be beautifully presented as well as delicious. Or in the summer months, it may have to be transported to a site in the middle of nowhere, so that a delicate pavlova decorated with carefully applied slices of fruit may not be as practical as a slab of old-fashioned fruitcake.

There is a very deep meaning to this sharing of food, but the first reason is certainly that it is pleasant, binds our pagan communities together, and reminds us of the bounty of the Goddess. The next is practical: attendees may have come a long way and need to be fed before they go home. My coven is quite far-flung, as in Cornwall the population density is one of the lowest in the UK, and coveners cannot always stay for supper when they have miles to go to get home. However, I always insist that they 'break bread' with the rest of us before they go – a simple bit of bread or other food and a mouthful of wine or juice, and they have satisfied the custom. In ancient times, hospitality was a sacred thing, and a man who robbed, harmed or killed someone who had been under his roof and eaten his bread and salt was considered beyond the pale. Even in the 21st century, food brings people together: businessmen schedule breakfast and lunch meetings, families meet up for meals, and children in the playground who do not get on might become more friendly after sharing sweets. Enjoying food has played a huge part in the stamping out of racial prejudice, as Indian, Chinese, Greek, Mexican, Thai, and many other ethnic minority people have introduced us to their wonderful cuisines. Food is a common language after all, and it is hard to hate someone who has just brought you a perfect crispy onion bhaji!

Another consideration is the appropriateness of the fare to the venue. For probably half of the Sabbats, you are potentially providing picnic food, rather than food which needs plates and cutlery. Whereas at Yule you might have a formal meal together, even at a restaurant, at Lughnasadh pagans would expect to be outside, at a sacred site, a stone circle or a sacred grove, even in someone's garden. As a coven high priestess of ten years' standing and a covener before that, I have enjoyed many a pleasant picnic in magical surroundings, from Iron Age hill forts to stone circles to holy wells, in company with hedge witches, Hermeticists, Heathens, Druids and Wiccans. While the biggest challenge is undoubtedly the dietary requirements of the attendees, whether that be due to health conditions or to the attendee preferring to refrain from certain foods for spiritual reasons, the next is how appropriate the food is to the venue. While some pagan groups go all out, carry a metal firepit or barbecue with them and are happy to cook up a hot meal, others may feel that finger food is more sensible for the occasion.

And, going back to diet choices, vegetarianism is one thing, but many pagans are hardline vegans, which means they will not use or eat any product that *exploits* or involves animals in any way, never mind requiring their death. This is due to the different way in which pagans regard animals, seeing them not as plastic-wrapped cutlets on the hoof but as fellow travellers on the planet, sons and daughters of the Goddess, just as we are.

Let me just confess that I am not a vegetarian: I tried it for a few years, and I was the most miserable failure. I longed for meat, and I cheated at every opportunity and for every excuse. But even more, I missed cooking with meat, using the skills I have acquired over 50 years of marriage to create delicious dishes for my family, even from cheaper cuts. Vegetarian food can be very dull; vegan food even more so. But over the years, I have learned to cook tasty and nourishing dishes for my coven, taking into consideration that we have a range of requirements from downright carnivores to hardline vegans. I have favourite recipes that I trot out regularly for certain festivals, and I also spend a lot of time trawling the Internet (thank Goddess for it!) for new ones.

Another resource is the tradition we were all brought up in: why not rifle through its food-based traditions for pagan ritual and pagan social occasions? You are not taking anything from the original culture, merely introducing it to a new set of no doubt appreciative diners! I was reared in a nominally Christian culture by two parents who wrote ‘C of E’ on the Census forms but never entered a church except for a friend’s wedding or a relative’s funeral, but of course I was exposed to full-on Christianity purely through being in the British education system from 1959 through to 1973, complete with assemblies, RE classes and carol services. Setting aside the claim you will often hear from pagans that “they stole it from us first”, my feeling about food is that it can’t be copyrighted … it is for everyone, like the air we breathe and the water we drink. Mince pies at pagan Yule? Why not, for Goddess’s sake? I suspect a true Christian (as opposed to a knee-jerk reactionary) would smile and be happy to give me their own recipe and maybe even give me a 'Blessed Yule' when I wished them a 'Merry Christmas'.

Many dishes already associated with other religions' festivals are very suitable for ours as well. Mince pies are a case in point: warm, spicy, and comforting, they are perfect food for a jolly timed for the winter solstice and probably just need a little tweaking of the recipe to make sure there is no lard, suet or other animal product in there that could offend a vegetarian (if you are not making your own, check the labels carefully). Hot cross buns – available all year round, just as though the supermarkets were on our side! – are associated with Christian Easter but perfectly designed for our own Midsummer, with their round shape and solar cross, and also a less messy finger food very suitable for carrying out to sacred sites, which is also a major consideration when you are planning what food contributions to take to an outdoor ritual.

That said, let us take a long and pleasant ramble through the culinary customs that have grown up around Neopaganism, particularly Wicca, and its eight festivals. In each case, I have tried to include suggestions on how to make the dish suitable for vegetarians, vegans and recovering alcoholics, if it is not already. Many of these dishes are also suitable for a coven supper after an Esbat or other get-together.

## THE SABBATS

### *Samhain*

**31st October–1st November.** Some streams celebrate this event at 15 degrees Scorpio, around 7th November, but

Wiccans acknowledge the liminal nature of this fire festival, which falls between one month and another, and in Celtic reckoning between one year and another, as the day after the festival (1st November) was considered New Year's Day. In Wicca, the Goddess claims Her ultimate power, moving into Her Crone aspect as winter sets in.

Samhain, better known to non-pagans as Halloween, is the festival of the dead, the date when all pagans turn their thoughts to their ancestors and their loved ones in spirit, a theme which also runs through many other cultures' sacred events at this time of year, from Remembrance Sunday in Europe to Dia de los Muertes in Mexico. At a Samhain ritual, you will commonly see photographs of loved ones on the altar, with flowers and tea lights in front of them, and hear prayers to them and for them, memories and wishes expressed by the attendees. There is always a box of tissues sitting handy at my own Samhain rituals.

However, the festival has another side. If the *veil* is thin, so that the beloved dead can return, then so also can the less than welcome visitors, the angry dead, the vengeful offended family spirits, the 'beasties', and the mischievous goblins and sprites. Our ancestors would have taken precautions against these, even as they left out light and food to welcome their loved ones. The ferocious grinning face of a carved pumpkin is a folk memory dating back to the turnip lanterns carved to scare away bad spirits, and dressing up in Halloween costumes harks back to the disguises worn by folks who were afraid that they might have offended their ancestors or feared an attack by evil entities of any kind, though the disguises might have been as simple as blacking or whitening their faces with soot or chalk and turning their clothes inside-out, a habit they possibly shared with Morris dancers, but for different reasons.

### *Samhain Fare*

The most famous dishes associated with Samhain are those crossing over directly from non-pagan Halloween traditions, to whit pumpkin pies, pumpkin bread and pumpkin soup, and dark spicy treats like gingerbread and spiced toffee. Rich dark food has a way of making you think of dark evenings and smoking fires. Apples are also a popular part of this seasonal cuisine, whether as pies, as toffee apples, or as the natural fruit.

While many attendees are happy to call in at their local supermarket and buy a pack of black and orange cupcakes decorated with spiders and bats, most pagans consider themselves to be closer to nature and to tradition than their non-pagan neighbours, and many share an interest in natural food, particularly free food they have gathered themselves from the hedgerow or have grown themselves. Add to this the percentage of pagans who are vegetarian or vegan, and you will find very little meat at a pagan celebration. What you will find is food that they consider appropriate to the season, often cooked with imagination and care.

#### PROSERPINE'S PUMPKIN SOUP

*This is probably the star of the show at any pagan event, especially if the weather is cold! I make my pumpkin soup this way:*

*You will need:*

1 medium-large orange pumpkin (try to leave buying it until the day, as they then drop in price, and I have seen them given away free in my local supermarket on Halloween day).
1 large onion.
2–3 cloves of fresh garlic
Oil, butter or vegan margarine (avoid butter if you have vegans in your gathering).
Salt.
Spices: I use 1 teaspoon of ginger and a little cinnamon for prosperity, black pepper and garlic for protection (necessary on this night!), and a little (*very* little! A pinch or the tip of a teaspoon) allspice, plus a teaspoon of turmeric to brighten the colour.

**METHOD:** First of all, you need to attack the pumpkin with a big sharp knife, hacking it in two or four and scooping out all the big flat seeds and the fibres they are nestled in. You can keep the seeds to plant next spring or use them in magic.

Brush the cut surfaces of the pumpkin with oil or melted butter or margarine, then place on a baking tray in the oven at around 200°C, or gas mark 6, for 40-50 minutes. When it comes out of the oven, it should look a little collapsed and have some browned edges. Set it aside to cool a little, enough to be able to handle it. Also keep any juices that have come out to add to the soup.

Peel and chop the onion, and put it into a large pan in which you have heated some oil, butter or margarine. Fry over a medium heat until transparent and fragrant, and add two or three garlic cloves, peeled and crushed or chopped. Once the whole lot is steaming away, you can add the spices. Start with a teaspoon of ground ginger (you can use peeled, finely chopped fresh ginger, but I don't think it gives as good a result). Add around half this quantity of ground cinnamon, then a very tiny pinch of allspice – be careful with this, as it is very strong. A few good whacks of freshly ground black pepper, and you're cooking with gas.

Now turn down the heat, and while this is simmering away, tackle the pumpkin. Now it is cooked, it will be a lot easier to peel off the orange skin, using a potato peeler or even just your fingers. If you miss a few bits, it won't matter too much, as it will be softened.

Once peeled, chop the pumpkin into rough chunks and add to the pan with about two pints of water – you can speed this up by having a boiling kettle ready.

Simmer for around 30 minutes, then pour into a liquidiser or blend with a stick blender until smooth and creamy. Season with salt to taste. You can turn this into quite a substantial meal by serving with it a separate bowl of grated cheese and homemade bread – much easier to make than most people realise.

## PLUTO'S PUNGENT PUMPKIN TAGINE

*This is a wonderfully warming dish, suitable for vegetarians and vegans, which you can serve if you've been out in the cold for the Sabbat. You don't need one of those fancy tall-lidded tagine dishes; an ordinary lidded pan will do just as well.*

*You will need:*

Olive oil.
1 large red onion (you can use a white onion, but it won't look as pretty).
A medium pumpkin, prepared.

1 can of chopped tomatoes in juice.
2 orange peppers (or red and yellow, if you can't find orange ones).
1 large aubergine, chopped.
3 fat cloves of garlic, peeled and crushed.
1 tablespoon of harissa paste, or more if you like it hot.
1 pack of apricots, the softer kind if possible, or you can soak them in hot water.
1 large cooking apple, peeled and cut into small chunks.
1 can of chickpeas (the black ones are very appropriate if you can find them).
Salt and freshly ground black pepper.
Fresh coriander leaves.

**METHOD:** Start by preparing your pumpkin, exactly as you did for the soup in the recipe above. Cut it into chunks when it is cool enough to handle.

Peel and chop the onion and start it frying in a large pan, adding the garlic and the harissa paste. When the onion is softened, add the canned tomatoes, the peppers, the aubergine, the pumpkin, the chickpeas, the apple, and the apricots, diluting the dish with a little water if it looks too thick. Season well with salt and lashings of ground black pepper. Cover with a lid and leave to simmer on a low heat for 20 minutes or so, until everything is tender and smells amazing. Toss a handful of chopped coriander leaves over and serve with crusty bread, rice, quinoa or couscous.

### SPOOKY SAMHAIN BLACK CAKE

*This is an invention of mine own, dear reader, yet I have encountered similar ideas elsewhere, often in Christmas recipe books, so it is not too outlandish an idea.*

*Basically, it is a rich fruitcake with the addition of treacle and dark chocolate to enhance its flavour and turn it even darker so that it tunes well with the season. This cake is not suitable for vegans, and if you are providing for a recovering alcoholic, omit the soaking in alcohol.*

*You will need:*

225g butter or margarine, at room temperature.
225g dark muscovado sugar.
2 tablespoons black treacle.
4 large eggs, room temperature, beaten.
285g self-raising flour.
200g bar of high cocoa solids dark chocolate.
About 500g dried fruit: raisins, sultanas, currants, prunes, stoned dates, even dried cranberries – whatever you like.
A glass of brandy or rum (optional).
1 tsp cinnamon.

**METHOD:** If you are using the alcohol, pour it into a bowl with all the dried fruit the day before you make the cake, and leave it to soak. Stir it every time you pass the bowl. The fruit will plump up and acquire a gorgeous flavour – but this may not be appropriate if you have anyone with issues around alcohol at the gathering.

The next day, grease and line a 9-inch deep-sided cake tin and heat the oven to 170°C, gas mark 4. Melt the chocolate in a bowl over a simmering pan of water, then set aside to cool slightly.

Using a large bowl and either a wooden spoon or an electric hand whisk, beat the butter, treacle, and sugar together until fluffy and lighter in colour. Add the egg a little at a time, sifting in a little of the flour if it looks as though it might curdle. Beat in the cooled but still liquid chocolate.

When it is all incorporated, lay down the whisk and fold the flour in carefully with a metal spoon. Add the soaked fruit and fold in until it is all amalgamated.

Turn into the prepared cake tin and place in the oven, not too near the top. Bake for around 1 hour 45 minutes, until a clean skewer inserted into the cake still comes out clean. It may need a little longer, as all ovens have their little ways, and you may need to lay a sheet of tinfoil over the top if it begins to turn too brown before the middle is cooked.

It really is too rich to need icing, but I like to sprinkle golden cake glitter* on the top before serving.

## YULE

**The Winter Solstice, around 21st December.** The solstice takes place as the sun enters Capricorn, so the date may vary from 19th to 23rd December and is celebrated by pagans as the beginning of the return of the sun, or the rebirth of the God. From here on, the days grow longer and the nights shorter. '*Yule*' is a Norse word which seems to mean 'wheel', as in 'the Wheel of the Year', and many ancient Norse customs will be instantly recognisable – as the Christians adopted them. So, the roasted meats and sweet goodies, the roaring fire, the carol singing, and the gifts are a very pagan way to celebrate.

* Can I just add that almost any cake is improved – to the eye, at any rate – by using cake glitter! This amazing edible fairy dust comes in every colour, including black! Sprinkle it onto spells for luck, healing, love, and prosperity. Like magician's flash paper – available online but always to be used with care by someone who knows what they are doing – it can also be used very effectively in ritual. You'll be surprised how much a witch can do with a little pot of this visual magic.

## *Yule Fare*

As with Christmas, red is a traditional colour at Yule, when it speaks of the sun and His rebirth. So red-coloured foods are often part of the menu at Yule celebrations, including things you would not necessarily see on a Christmas table, like beetroot and pomegranate, but also, of course, cranberries, which the immortal Delia popularised as a Christmas ingredient some 35 years ago. Roasted meats are an important part of Yule (except, of course, for vegetarians and vegans), with roast pork being particularly important at Yule for followers of Freyr, whose sacred animal is the pig. Preserved fruits, which would once have been the only way of enjoying fruit this deep into the winter and would have been hoarded for the occasion, have always played an important role at Christmas and are also very traditional at Yule. The other big Yule ingredient is, as with Christmas, spices. Food needs to be hearty, warming and comforting!

### MOTHER HOLLE'S MUSHROOM PÂTÉ

*This makes a delicious festive vegan starter but is also quite portable so it can be taken to outdoor rituals at other times of year – and it freezes! If you pick your own mushrooms, I can only say: be careful! But some of our meatier wild mushrooms, such as field mushrooms, puffballs, the parasol mushroom (Macrolepiota procera) and the chicken of the woods (Laetiporus sulphureus), would be very suitable for this dish. You can turn up the volume a little by using butter for the cooking, adding cream cheese to the mix, and grating Parmesan cheese over the top, when it will still be suitable for vegetarians.*

*You will need:*

100g mushrooms: these can be button, open cap, chestnut, chanterelles, or even porcini (rehydrated if they are dried). If they are foraged, pick them over well, discard any that look bruised or worm-eaten and wash them well.
1 large onion, very finely chopped.
2 fat cloves of garlic, crushed.
About 100g vegan margarine.
Grated zest of an orange.
Pepper and salt.
1 heaped teaspoon of thyme, fresh if possible, chopped.
Tiny pinch of allspice, if liked, for that Yule fragrance.

**METHOD:** Melt some of the butter in a pan and add the onion and the crushed garlic. Chop the mushrooms finely, and add them, and also the spices, the zest and the thyme (I feel it has to be thyme, our most basic herb, which also grows wild in the UK). Cook the mixture quite slowly until all is tender, and then place in a food processor and blend, as smooth as you want it (you may have to spoon out some of the liquid that comes out of the mushrooms first). Season to taste. Turn into a dish (a freezer-proof one if making ahead), let it set a little and pour the rest of the butter or margarine over the top to seal it. Garnish with a sprig of thyme and serve with toast or savoury biscuits.

## HEARTY LENTIL AND CRANBERRY YULE ROAST

*This recipe has it all for vegetarians and vegans at Yule: delicious nut roast studded with jewel-red cranberries and seasoned with spices and savoury herbs. It will tempt even the meat eaters!*

*You will need:*

300g lentils: you can use all red or all green, or a mixture.
150g toasted chopped nuts, either mixed, or cashews or even peanuts.
1 onion.
3 fat cloves of garlic.
1 small pack of dried cranberries, or use 100g fresh cranberries, which are in the shops at Yule.
2 teaspoons of dried sage.
A small pinch of allspice.
A small pinch of chilli powder, if liked.
An inch cube of fresh root ginger, peeled and grated.
A good handful of chopped parsley, plus some to garnish.
1 heaped tablespoon of tomato puree.
1 tablespoon gram (chickpea) flour, or you can use plain flour.
Oil.
Pepper and salt.
3 tablespoons of cranberry sauce – the kind that has pieces of fruit in it works best.

**METHOD:** Pour boiling water over the lentils and soak, preferably overnight. Preheat the oven to 200°C, gas mark 6, and line and grease an eight-inch cake tin.

Cook the lentils over a low heat until soft, mashing them with a spoon as they cook until you have a nice soft puree – it doesn't need to be completely smooth, but should be reasonably dry, so be careful how much water you add.

Peel and finely chop the onion and the garlic, and fry in another pan in some oil on a low heat until soft. Add the nuts, cranberries, herbs and spices, and fry gently for another minute. Turn off the heat and add the lentils, tomato purée and gram flour, stirring everything together well, and seasoning with salt and pepper. Spoon into the prepared tin and press it down lightly to give a nice flat top.

Bake in the preheated oven for 40 mins. Leave to cool for a short time, then turn out onto a plate. While it is still hot, spread the cranberry sauce over the top and decorate with a sprig of holly or a sprinkle of chopped parsley.

### DIANE'S YULE CHUTNEY

*Diane in this case is not the moon Goddess, but a small and adorable flesh-and-blood goddess who belongs to my coven, and who once made this chutney for me and was then kind enough to give me the recipe ... I have never made any other kind since. If you grow tomatoes, it is a splendid way to use any glut, and you can freeze the fruits if you don't have time to make it straight away. As you can see, it is suitable for vegans and vegetarians.*

*You will need:*

900g tomatoes, chopped small.
225g raisins.**
225g red onions, chopped.
1 garlic clove, crushed.
1 heaped teaspoon of ground ginger or (preferably) 2 balls of preserved ginger, chopped.
The grated zest of an orange.
Chopped apricots or cranberries (optional).
Sprinkle of coarse-ground black pepper.
225g caster or demerara sugar.
600ml vinegar (any kind: sherry, wine, malt, or cider).

** You can use other fruit instead of raisins – i.e., sultanas, dates or apples – but I find that raisins work best. Makes about 6 small jam jars full.

**METHOD:** Place the chopped tomatoes in a large pan, add the raisins and other fruit, onions, garlic, and caster sugar. Pour the vinegar into the pan and bring the mixture to the boil. Simmer for two hours, uncovered, until soft and thickened. Transfer the chutney to warmed sterilized jars (sterilised in a warm oven for about 1.5 hours). Put on the lids, leave to cool, and store in a cool, dark place to mature for one month. The chutney will keep unopened for up to one year. Once opened, store them in the fridge.

This tracklement works very well with the Yule lentil roast above, and the filled and decorated jars also make lovely Yule presents.

## IMBOLC

**31st January–1st February.** Or in some traditions, 15 degrees Aquarius, or around 7th February. Imbolc celebrates the first signs of spring – which is why you almost always see snowdrops on pagan altars at this time: these brave little flowers are always the first things to rear their heads, often poking through the snow. Our forebears would have been celebrating the first births of livestock on the farms and the subsequent availability of milk as a welcome addition to the meagre winter diet. Imbolc or Oimelc (both pronounced roughly 'Immolk') are said to mean 'in the belly' and 'ewes' milk'. Either way, this Sabbat is strongly associated with milk, which may be served in the Cup at rituals instead of the usual wine.

### *Imbolc Fare*

I'm afraid vegans have a thin time of it when it comes to Imbolc food, as the emphasis is firmly on dairy foods, especially milk – but also eggs, as those breeds of chicken which have not been bred to lay all year round will start laying again around Imbolc. However, with the cornucopia of vegan-friendly dairy alternatives now available, you can still include them by offering nut or seed milks, tofu and other non-dairy foods. And if 'proper cow juice' is served in the Cup, they can touch their lips to the rim without drinking, as I do (I can't bear milk), or a second Cup filled with a dairy alternative drink could be offered.

### SPRING SPANAKOPITA FOR VEGANS

*Spanakopita is a delicious, finger-friendly 'pie' from Greece which normally includes egg and feta cheese – and you can still follow the classic recipe if you don't have vegans to cater for, as its dairy content makes it very appropriate for Imbolc. However, the cheese and egg can be replaced with vegetable foods and can be almost as delicious. I added sundried tomatoes to this to make it more tasty.*

*You will need:*

1-2 packs filo pastry (check it has the green leafy vegan 'V' sign).
1 jar sundried tomatoes (with the jars of antipasto in the supermarket).
1 large onion.
2-3 fat cloves of garlic, crushed or chopped.
500g frozen spinach, thawed and squeezed as dry as possible.
Large tub of hummus or 2 cans of any kind of soft beans.
A big bunch of parsley.
Pepper and salt.

**METHOD:** Preheat the oven to 160°C, gas mark 3. Open the filo pastry and cover with a damp tea-towel. Grease a large dish thoroughly. You won't need any extra oil for this recipe, as the sundried tomatoes come in oil to which they have imparted their delicious, fruity, savoury flavour. Drain the jar, reserving the oil.

Chop the onion, garlic, sundried tomatoes, parsley (stalks and all) and spinach, and put it all in a bowl with a good glug of the tomato oil. Season with salt and lots of black pepper and mix thoroughly. Mix in a large tub of hummus, or you can use any kind of soft canned beans, well mashed.

Now start to line the dish with sheets of filo, well brushed with oil – use the oil from the sundried tomatoes for a better flavour. Leave some overhang at the sides of the dish.

Tip the filling into the lined dish and then fold over the filo sheets and add more until you have a tidy 'pie', brushing with oil as you go.

Bake for one hour. When it is cooled, this sets reasonably firmly and is not too messy to eat without plates.

### LADY WILLOW'S 'SPRING IS COMING' SEEDY CAKE

*This is a very old-fashioned cake, a favourite with the Victorians, which many older people do not like, as they remember being given it and disliking it as children! Which you can understand when you know that it is flavoured with caraway, which is quite astringent and bitter, and very much an adult flavour. The seeds tie it to either Imbolc or Ostara, and the white icing to Imbolc, so it is suitable for either Sabbat. This is vegetarian-friendly, but cannot really be made without eggs, although you could have a shot at making it as a banana loaf, simply replacing the eggs with a couple of well-ripened bananas.*

*You will need:*

175g butter or margarine.
175g golden caster sugar.
3 free-range eggs.
250g self-raising flour.
2 tablespoons of milk.
2 tablespoons of caraway seeds (adjust to your taste accordingly).
150g icing sugar.
Juice and grated zest of 1 lemon.

**METHOD:** Preheat your oven to 175°C, gas mark 4. Beat the butter/margarine and sugar together in a bowl until they are light and fluffy.

Add in the free-range eggs SLOWLY. Once the eggs are fully blended, fold in the flour and the caraway seeds using a metal spoon. Place the mixture into a greased 2 lb loaf tin. Place it in the preheated oven and bake for 45 mins. Check that the middle of the cake has baked – do the skewer thing if you're not sure.

Once baked, leave to cool in the tin for 10 to 15 minutes and then turn out onto a cooling rack.

Lady Willow's recipe is light, fluffy and delicious, but you can also ice the seed cake with lemon icing, which counteracts the slight bitterness of the seeds and brings a sharp sweetness to the cake. When the cake is thoroughly cool, mix the lemon juice into the icing sugar, just enough to make a spreadable but stiffish icing that won't drip down the sides. Sprinkle the lemon zest on top, or you could sprinkle a few more caraway seeds, either looks very nice.

## SPICY SPRING PANEER AND SPINACH

*Paneer is a simple cheese made in India – where they have a lot of cows! Out of this resource has grown their amazing repertoire of milk puddings and milky or yoghurty drinks, some of which have also become very popular in the UK. Making paneer is quite a long process, but if you have a fridge, a Thermos flask, and a square of muslin, you can do it easily. Or you can substitute tofu, which would then make this suitable for vegans as well as vegetarians.*

*You will need:*

500ml Greek-style plain yoghurt, or 1 pint of milk (whole milk is best), and a very small amount of plain yoghurt.
500g spinach, fresh or frozen.
1 onion, chopped.
3 cloves of garlic, crushed or chopped.
1 can chopped tomatoes.
100g mushrooms, chopped.
1 red or orange pepper, sliced.
Spices: I recommend garam masala, turmeric, cumin, coriander, black pepper, and a little cinnamon, or you can just use shop-bought curry powder.
Salt.

**METHOD:** First make your paneer, which you will need to start two days before. Warm a pint of milk in a pan (not too hot!) and pour it into a Thermos. Add a tablespoon of plain yoghurt, shake, and leave overnight. Or if you are short of time, buy a 500ml pot of plain Greek-style yoghurt.

In the morning, tip out your yoghurt (which should be thickened and smell nice) into a square of muslin in a sieve over a pan or wide jug. Leave overnight again, in the fridge this time (you see, it doesn't take much time to do, but does need foresight ...).

Fry the onion and garlic in the oil until transparent and starting to have golden brown edges. Add the spices and continue to fry: they will start to give off their wonderful aroma. Add the sliced peppers and chopped mushrooms and continue to cook until tender.

Now add the tomatoes and the spinach: if using fresh spinach, you will need to let it wilt down, but if frozen, it must be thawed before cooking. Mix it all thoroughly, ensuring that the spices are well mixed in with every ingredient. Season with salt to taste.

Now slice up your paneer into chunks and add them to the dish, mixing them in carefully. They will break up but will still look and taste nice. Serve with rice or couscous.

## OSTARA

**The Spring Equinox, usually around 21st March.** The sun enters Taurus some time between 19th and 23rd March, and Ostara is celebrated much as the Christians celebrate Easter, as a step on the way to full spring and summer, with bunnies (actually, the hare is the animal associated with this festival), eggs, daffodils, and lots of hope and planning. At this time, the length of the days equals the length of the nights, as its name explains. The festival marks the coming together of the Goddess and God as They fall in love, and Their union fertilises the earth.

## *Ostara Fare*

Seeds and eggs – both potent symbols of the returning spring, fertility, birth and rebirth – obviously play a significant role in the foods for this festival. Again, vegans could lose out at many celebrations, which are centred on eggs, but Ostara foods also include many vegan-friendly alternatives like seeds, sprouted seeds, and nuts. Or you could create 'eggs' made from non-animal protein. Supermarkets now sell vegetarian and vegan 'scotch eggs' and other vegan dishes based on egg recipes, but really all you need to do is shape a vegan food substance – such as falafel – into an egg shape.

### FLORA'S FLAVOURSOME FALAFEL

*'Falafel' is a fairly general term for a bean patty flavoured with spices and herbs and deep-fried – the familiar Indian onion bhaji is technically a falafel. Originating in Egypt, they are enjoyed all over the Middle East (and here as well!). This recipe is suitable for Ostara, as it is deep green when broken open – a conjuring of the summer to come …*

*Gram (chickpea) flour is now easily obtainable in supermarkets in the 'ethnic' aisles, next to Basmati rice and curry pastes. It is far better for this recipe than actual chickpeas, as it is dry and binds the mixture together.*

*You will need:*

About 150g gram flour.
1 teaspoon salt.
1 level teaspoon baking powder.
1 large onion.

2 garlic cloves.
1 bunch of fresh coriander.
1 bunch of parsley.
Green things: I save ends of green peppers, parsley stalks, celery leaves, etc. in a bag in the freezer to make falafel – pagans don't believe in waste! You need about a double handful.
Spices: you can use what you like and experiment, as many spices work well in this dish, but I use coriander and cumin (1 teaspoon of each) with a lot of black pepper and a pinch of chilli powder.
Oil for frying.

**METHOD:** This is best done in a food processor, but you can chop everything by hand. Put the quartered onion and the peeled garlic into the 'pro and blitz until evenly chopped. Now add the green vegetables and herbs, stalks and all, and blitz again: it should be quite finely chopped. It should already be smelling amazing.

Pour the oil into a deep frying pan or thick-bottomed saucepan: it needs to be at least 6cm deep. Turn on the heat under your oil, but make sure you don't forget about it and overheat it.

Turn the chopped ingredients out into a large bowl and add the gram flour, salt, spices, and baking powder, mixing carefully until you have a nice stiff mixture that you can form into balls easily. If it gets too stiff, add a little warm water: the looser the mixture, the softer the falafel.

With wet hands, form the mixture into little eggs – make them the same size as eggs – and place them into the hot oil, moving them about so they fry on all sides. When they are quite a dark golden colour, they will be done inside, and you can remove them onto a plate lined with kitchen paper to drain. If you like, you can serve them in little 'nests' of shredded lettuce, or even more appropriately, of sprouted seeds – to underline the spring connection. Delicious hot or cold.

## EOSTRE EGGY FLANLETS

*This is a very simple dish, but none the worse for that. It is a sort of finger food version of a traditional pie and a very good way of bringing eggs into the feast. There is no easy way of making this one vegan, I'm afraid, but it will be a hit with the vegetarians!*

*Most supermarket eggs are unfertilised, so you can eat these without feeling that you have wronged a hen by eating her babies – but if you wish, you can formally thank the chicken for her sacrifice as you prepare the eggs.*

*You will need:*

200g + 30g self-raising flour.
100g + 30g butter or margarine.
250g grated Cheddar cheese.
2 teaspoons mustard powder.
6 eggs.
300ml milk.
1 tablespoon of chopped parsley.
Pepper and salt.

**METHOD:** First make the filling. Hard-boil the eggs for about 6 minutes, then plunge into cold water to cool before peeling them. Melt the 30g of butter gently in a pan, then add the 30g of flour and one teaspoonful of the mustard powder. Stir them together and begin adding the milk, a little at a time, stirring well to prevent lumps forming.

When the sauce is nice and thick, stir in most of the cheese, leaving about 50g to sprinkle on top. Stir in the chopped parsley and season, and set aside to cool a little.

Rub the 200g of flour with 1 teaspoon of mustard powder and the butter together with your hands to the 'breadcrumb' stage, then draw together with a little cold water. Rest in the fridge for a while.

While the pastry is chilling, grease a 12-portion patty tin, the kind you might make jam tarts in, and preheat the oven to 200°C, gas mark 6.

Take the pastry from the fridge, roll it out on a floured board and cut rounds with the largest pastry cutter (these tend to come in a set of three) and pop one in each hole in the patty tin, pressing gently down to form the base of the tarts.

Now to bring it all together: slice all the eggs in half lengthways and lay one half in each pastry base, cut-side down: you may need to trim off some of the white at the 'pointy' end to make them fit. Carefully pour in the cheese sauce, making sure each egg is covered but the tart is not too full, or it will overflow. Put a little grated cheese on top of each one. Put in the oven for about 15 minutes (keep an eye on them!) until the pastry is golden and the cheese has also crisped and gone golden brown. Very good hot or cold, but I'm afraid these do not freeze well because of the hard-boiled eggs, which can go very tough and rubbery in the freezer.

## SPRING SEEDED BREAD

*Bread, as I have already said, is easy! All you have to do is bear in mind that the yeast is a living creature and needs its comforts before it can work for you. Don't put the dough in a hot place, as the yeast will be unhappy. It needs to be warm like a cat: so the kitchen dresser, rather than the top of the stove.*

*It is very simple to make your bread suitable for the equinox festival – and super delicious – by tarting it up with seeds. Smaller seeds like poppy, sunflower, and sesame are suitable for the inside of the bread, while harder, larger seeds like pumpkin and flax look very inviting on top. When choosing your ingredients, keep in mind that lard or dairy products render the bread unsuitable for vegans – oil or vegan margarine should be used instead.*

*You will need:*

500g strong white flour.
1 sachet dried yeast (you can do it the hard way with live yeast if you like!).
1 teaspoon of salt.
Oil or fat of some kind: butter, lard, vegan margarine or dairy cream (I always keep any leftover cream in the freezer for bread-making).
Seeds: pine nuts, pumpkin seeds, flax seeds, poppy seeds, sunflower seeds ... your choice. Most supermarkets sell mixed seeds too.
1 teaspoon of vinegar (this is a hack!).
Hand-hot water or milk.

**METHOD:** Put the flour and salt in a large bowl and add the seeds. I would start with two or three tablespoons of seeds, but you can use your own judgement if you think it needs more. Now add the fat. This should be about 50g of solid fats like margarine or lard, which should be rubbed in first, or about 2–3 tablespoons of oil. Add the teaspoon of vinegar. This adds a touch of acidity to the dough, which the yeast likes and which will help it rise. Sprinkle the dried yeast over the top and start adding the warm milk or water, a little at a time, working it in with your fingers or processing it in a machine. Do not add enough liquid to make it sloppy: the dough should be easy to handle and should lose its stickiness as you work and become silky. Knead it well for about five minutes.

When the dough is ready, lay it on a floured board and shape it as you wish. I often plait my dough, as this makes the loaf easy for everyone at a ritual to pull a piece off without needing a knife. Simply tease the dough into a long fat roll and cut it lengthwise into three fat snakes, leaving them still joined at one end. Then plait these together and press together with a drop of water at the other end.

Place the loaf on a lined or greased tray and leave in a warm place to rise. This may take some time, but you will suddenly notice that it has doubled in size and looks right. Heat your oven to very hot: 225°C, gas mark 7, and meanwhile decorate the loaf with the exterior seeds by painting the top with warm water and sprinkling them on – the water ensures that they stick.[***]

Place in the hot oven, and after about five minutes turn the heat down below 200°C, gas mark 6, and bake for about 25–30 minutes. When it is done, it should sound hollow when tapped.

## BELTANE

**30th April–1st May.** Or in some traditions, 15 degrees Taurus, or around 7th May. However, in the UK, May Day

*** Note: if you find your topping seeds burn, you can add them halfway through the baking process instead of at the beginning.

has always been celebrated, with maypoles, Morris dancers and other ancient pagan customs – despite the efforts of the Church to stamp them out.

In Wicca, this is the marriage day of the Goddess and God – which makes it a popular choice for handfastings (pagan marriages).

## *Beltane Fare*

Honey and mead are especially relevant to Beltane because of their association with love and marriage, and also foods made with honey. There is a lot of food to choose from at Beltane, when the earth is in full flower and offering her bounty in so many ways. It's too early for most fruits, but there is an abundance of green things like herbs and early vegetables, and of course there is always baking!

Honey is a bit of a *sine qua non* at Beltane, and there are alternatives you can use in any recipe, which will make it suitable for vegans and still delicious. Golden syrup is very useful in place of honey, as is maple syrup, with its aromatic, smoky flavour.

### THE MARRIAGE OF HEAVEN HONEY DRINK

*No need for recovering alcoholics or designated drivers to feel left out when others are quaffing mead at Beltane rituals. This beverage combines the sweetness of honey with herbal flavours and even a hint of bitterness to give a satisfying drink that does not feel as though it came from the children's squash aisle at the supermarket. Not suitable for vegans, although you could substitute maple syrup for the honey. However, some of the herbs will not go well with this, and you might need to experiment to find others that will marry well with it. Experiment anyway: obviously, oniony herbs like chives and garlic will not be suitable, but many others – and sweet spices too – will work. If you collect and dry elderflowers in the summer, these will be a magical addition to the drink, or you can use a cordial, as below.*

*You will need:*

100g runny honey.
½ litre of water.
3-4 bay leaves.
A sprig of rosemary.
2 sprigs of thyme (lemon thyme is nice).
2 or 3 sage leaves.
3 sprigs of basil.
3 tablespoons of elderflower cordial.

**METHOD:** Bring the water to a boil in a pan and add the herbs. Turn off the heat and let them steep for an hour, then reheat and strain the water onto the honey in a bowl, stirring well. Add the elderflower cordial and mix well. This is very pleasant hot or served cold over ice.

### BELTANE BAKLAVA BAGUETTE

*This is a no-fuss version of the favourite Greek dessert, but instead of filo pastry, which is quite difficult to use and often to find as well, I have substituted puff pastry, which makes for lovely fluffy little slices which don't shatter as you eat them. As it uses honey, baklava is not for vegans, but here I have suggested a way of making a vegan version.*

*You will need:*

A block of puff pastry (check for the vegan symbol if necessary).
About 200g chopped mixed nuts: pistachios are traditional but very expensive, so I tend to substitute walnuts.
2 tablespoons white sugar.
1 teaspoon ground cardamom (or any sweet spice you prefer).
3 tablespoons of runny honey OR maple syrup.
½ tablespoon of lemon juice.
1 tablespoon of orange flower water or rose water.
Cornflour (optional).

**METHOD:** Line a large baking tray with non-stick parchment and preheat the oven to 180°C, gas mark 5.

Roll out the pastry on a floured board, or you can often buy ready-rolled pastry, which might just need a few tweaks to make it thin enough. You are aiming to have a long rectangle about 5mm thick. When it is ready, lay it on a damp tea-towel.

Mix the nuts with the sugar in a bowl and add the spices, flavourings, lemon juice and honey or maple syrup. If the mixture looks too runny, add a little cornflour and mix well.

Using a palette knife, spread the nut and spice mixture all over the pastry, leaving about 3cms bare along each edge. Now brush a little warm water along all four sides of the pastry and carefully roll the pastry up from one side, using the tea-towel, as if you were making a Swiss roll. Press the final dampened edge against the pastry roll and pinch the ends together to seal well.

Place in the hot oven and cook for around 25 minutes, then decrease the temperature to 150°C, gas mark 3, for a further 20 minutes, until golden and puffy. Remove from the oven and dust with icing sugar. Leave to cool, and cut into slices.

### BELTANE LOVE-BOMBS

*Not too extreme a name for these chocolate oatcakes, which are related to the things we used to make in primary school from cornflakes or rice krispies and melted chocolate, this last ingredient being now quite as inextricably associated with love as honey. Oats are a food of Beltane, and perhaps a little more natural and healthy than breakfast cereal. The original recipe called for golden syrup – which would make it acceptable for vegans – but I have swapped it for honey, which is appropriate for Beltane. You can always change it back again.*

*You will need:*

200g milk chocolate.
2 tablespoons of honey, set or runny.
50g butter.
200g rolled oats.
Pinch of salt.

**METHOD:** These could not be easier; in fact we all remember making them in school under the watchful eye of Mrs Jenkins, the Year Two teacher, don't we?

Heat the chocolate, butter and honey very gently in a large pan (to save on the washing up) until just melted. Add the pinch of salt – which makes a surprising difference – and then tip in the oats and mix until everything is coated with the chocolate and honey.

Now you can either dollop the mixture into individual cupcake cases, like we did at school, or turn it into a greased and lined tin and pop it in the fridge. When it is set, cut into squares.

Of course, this is quite a simple, plain recipe, and you can do all sorts to make the cakes more festive for Beltane: add miniature marshmallows or dried or candied fruit or some of those tiny pastel sugar shapes meant for sprinkling on cupcakes – hearts would be appropriate. Anyway, they may be easy and simple to make, but I betcha don't take any home!

## MIDSUMMER

**The Summer Solstice, around 21st June.** The solstice takes place as the sun enters Cancer, so it may vary from around the 19th to the 23rd June, marking the very height of the sun's power and the point at which it begins to decline, the days becoming shorter and the nights longer. Rituals taking place around this time are usually aimed at encouraging the God to stay just a little longer so that the harvests might ripen and the cold of winter might be delayed, but also at thanking Him for the summer and for His eventual sacrifice.

### *Midsummer Fare*

Any food associated with this sun festival should be joyous and golden, and here we must pause to thank the Christians for their wonderful hot-cross buns, which may have been pagan originally but are still with us because of their association with Good Friday. They make a very appropriate treat at Midsummer, being decorated with a solar cross and often tinted yellow as well. Saffron buns are also yellow and a very good idea at Midsummer.

Early summer fruits (notably strawberries!) and garden vegetables are all appropriate for Midsummer, as are crystallised flowers, especially rose petals. Any golden or yellow foods such as sweetcorn, eggs, cheese and butter would be good, and actually there is nothing nicer at a Midsummer after-ritual feast than an old-fashioned quiche, especially if you 'dye' the egg mixture with a little turmeric before baking.

### GRÁINNE'S GOLDENHEART PASTIES

*Vegetarian/vegan. When these are broken open to eat, the glorious golden colour makes them a treat for the eyes as well as the mouth.*

*You will need:*

Pasty pastry made with 500g strong (bread) white flour and 250g vegetable fat.
1 large onion, peeled and chopped.
2 large potatoes, peeled and diced.
4 large carrots, peeled and diced.
1 teaspoon of turmeric.
Oil.
120g grated strong Cheddar cheese (omit or replace it with pureed red lentils to make the pasties vegan).
Chives or spring onions.
Salt and pepper.

**METHOD:** Steam or boil the potato and carrot until just tender. Fry the onion in a little oil until transparent, add the turmeric and the cooked veg, and stir well. Add the grated cheese, if using, and chopped chives, and then mix. Set aside to cool slightly.

Make the pasty pastry. The easiest way is to pop the fat into the freezer for 10 mins, and then grate it into the flour and add a teaspoon of salt. Use some cold water to draw it all together, as with shortcrust pastry.

Roll out the pasty pastry into rounds and heap the filling on the centre. Turn over and crimp the edges to seal, brushing them with a bit of water first. Bake for 20 mins at 200°C, gas mark 6. Makes 4 large or 6 medium, or you could make what we call in Cornwall 'pixie pasties', in which case, you would get around 10.

## CRIMSON GLORIES

*Vegetarian/vegan. I have actually served these as a starter for dinner parties, but they are just as good cold, and the red colour ties them to the sun and Midsummer, though orange peppers are almost as good. Buy big 'four-barrelled' peppers.*

*You will need:*

3 medium aubergines.
3 tablespoons olive oil.
1 large clove of garlic, chopped or crushed.
Juice of 1 large lemon.
3 tablespoons of chopped parsley.
Salt and pepper.
4 large red peppers.
A handful of grated Cheddar cheese (optional).

**METHOD:** Grill the aubergines until the skins are all blackened, then cool slightly. Run under the tap to remove skins. Liquidise with the oil and add the flavourings.

Halve and core the peppers lengthwise, cutting through the stalks as well to give a good shape. Brush the insides generously with oil, and bake for 20 mins at 180°C.

Fill the peppers with the aubergine mixture and return to the oven for 20 minutes to heat through. You can top with cheese if you like.

### LADY ELEN'S SOLSTICE SHORTBREAD

*These yummy biscuits perfectly reflect the image of the sun rising on the eastern horizon around 4.45am on Midsummer's Day. My high priest Karen (her tenure goes back to a time before we had any males in the coven to take on this role) turns these out for all sorts of occasions, often with fresh strawberries. These delicious treats are also very appropriate for the winter solstice – mince pies are all very well but often contain suet, which is a no-no for anyone vegetarian or vegan. These cookies, however, are not only vegan but also a feast for the eyes as well as the mouth.*

*You will need:*

180g plain white flour.
120g vegan margarine.
60g caster sugar.
Pinch of salt.
A bar of high cocoa solids plain chocolate (look for vegan chocolate).

**METHOD:** Preheat the oven to 180°C and line or grease a baking sheet.

Cream the margarine and sugar together with a wooden spoon until pale and fluffy, then lay aside the wooden spoon and sift the flour and salt into the bowl, mixing together lightly with a metal spoon. Draw the dough together with your hands, then roll out on a floured board to about half a centimetre thick and use a circular cookie cutter (a plain, not a fluted one) to make rounds until you have used it all up. Lay the cookies on the baking sheet and bake for around 20 minutes, or until light golden and slightly risen. Leave to cool.

Break up the chocolate in a small bowl and melt over a pan of simmering water. This can take ages, as you can't use boiling water, but I find starting the chocolate off in the microwave helps a lot.

When you have a nice bowl of melted chocolate, dip your cookies in carefully until you have one half covered in chocolate – try to get a nice straight line across the middle of the biscuits. Lay each one down on a sheet of non-stick paper to set. If you like, you can sprinkle gold glitter on the bare halves (using a piece of kitchen paper to mask the chocolate half) to look even more like the sun. You can also flavour the dough while mixing it, with almond or vanilla essence or cinnamon.

## LUGHNASADH

**31st July–1st August.** Or in some traditions, 15 degrees Leo, or around 7th August.

Lughnasadh is our first harvest festival (paganism has three in the year) and celebrates the gathering of grain. The name ties it to the Celtic God Lugh or Llew, but it is more about his foster mother Tailtiu, who died from exhaustion after single-handedly clearing the land and planting it to feed her people. Lugh held games in her honour – which you will sometimes see today at pagan gatherings for this festival.

## *Lughnasadh Fare*

This Sabbat is about gratitude and celebration, and you will find plenty of cider and beer being splashed around with more solid fare. This is a time when pagans think about their achievements through the year and offer their thanks to the Gods for them, so any food considered a celebration food is appropriate. Why not champagne, as drunk after personal 'harvests'? Or in Cornwall, *hevva* (heavy) cake – traditionally prepared by housewives when their men came into port with a catch: you can have it on the table in 30 minutes, and its criss-cross scoring, representing fishing nets, and currants as fish, speak of old sympathetic magic. Another Cornish tradition, Stargazy pie, has the same resonance.

However, grain and its main product, bread, are the heart and soul of this Sabbat, and no high priestess worth her salt would fail to provide bread for it – hopefully homemade and even still warm from her oven! Bread is a lot easier to make than many people realise. You may read a recipe, and it talks about activating the yeast, 'knocking back' and 're-proving' and other arcane terms ... pshaw! I don't do any of these things, yet I always get compliments on my bread. Be clever: take shortcuts, buy easy yeast, and make sure time is on your side. There are some little hacks you can use as well, which I included in the first bread recipe.

Bread is not only a very suitable food and offering for Lughnasadh but can certainly be used for other rituals as well. You can even colour it with the right correspondences! When I was working as a WI cookery judge in Wiltshire, there was one village show I attended regularly where an exhibitor used to enter dyed bread: she had obviously added food colouring at the mixing stage, and the result was bright blue or bright green or bright yellow bread. I have to say, I was not impressed: it looked nasty, and the strange colour rather put you off appreciating the flavour. But it could certainly work as part of a ritual, perhaps with blue bread for a water rite or yellow for a Midsummer ritual. Or you could make sure the colour was achieved through the use of natural ingredients: a tablespoon of turmeric in the mix would give you a bright yellow-gold bread which would not look too strange to eat but would be perfect for any sun ritual such as Midsummer or Lughnasadh. Many fruits and vegetables have naturally bright colours and can be used to enhance bread, as in the recipe below.

### TAILTIU'S HARVEST SUNDRIED TOMATO AND BASIL BREAD

*Vegan. Sundried tomatoes are available in all larger supermarkets (or online), and they achieve a level of yumminess which far outstrips ordinary tomato paste. It's a holiday taste.*

*You will need:*

500g strong white flour.
1 sachet dried yeast (or you can do it the hard way with live yeast if you like!).
1 teaspoon salt.
A 285g jar of sundried tomatoes or a 185g jar of sundried tomato puree.
If using the puree, add about 2 tablespoons of olive oil.
A bunch of fresh basil, finely chopped (you can use dried).
1 teaspoon of vinegar.
Hand-hot water.

**METHOD:** If you are lucky enough to have a stand-mixer or a breadmaker, this will be even easier, but you can do it by hand, which gives you an opportunity to put spoken charms into the dough as you knead it, to bless those who are going to eat it.

Put all the dry ingredients into a large bowl and add the chopped basil and the sundried tomatoes. Use your own judgement on whether you add all the oil from the jar, as not everyone likes very oily bread. Personally, I do, as it makes it very rich and flavoursome. Add in the vinegar and start adding the hot water – which should not be too hot to put your hand in – mixing it as you go. If you spread out your fingers, you can use your hand like a sort of whisk to bring the dough together. Add only just enough water to achieve this. The dough should be sticky but never sloppy, and as you go on mixing and kneading (which you should continue with for at least five minutes), it will lose its stickiness and become silky and elastic.

The dough should now be a fairly uniform tomato-orange colour, with green flecks from the herbs and the occasional lump of tomato. Shape it carefully into a loaf and lay it aside for an hour or so until it has doubled in size. I usually form mine into a plait, as this means you do not need a knife to serve it and guests can just easily pull away sections – useful if you are at a sacred site and not near your kitchen drawer.

Heat the oven to 200°C, gas mark 6, and bake the bread for around 35 mins. Keep checking it – it won't fall like a cake if you open the door – and take it out when it looks a lovely brown colour. Give it a sharp tap, and if it is done, it will sound hollow.

## SACRED SACRIFICE SALAD

*Vegan. A good hearty harvest salad can be all you need on the table, apart from some nice crusty bread and maybe a little salad dressing. If you base it on something a bit solid, like grains or a small-shaped pasta such as conchigliette, orzo or orecchiette, and take care to include as many flavours, textures and colours as possible, it will be sure to draw some 'oohs' from the pagans as you set it down.*

**METHOD:** Start with your base of carbohydrates, of which you will need about 200g for a medium group of diners. I use bulgur wheat or quinoa, as I find couscous turns into a rubber mat as soon as it is cooked unless you drench it in a gallon of oil. Cook it as usual in salted boiling water until just tender.

While the grain or pasta is cooking, start on the vegetables. I recommend any or all of these: red onions, cherry tomatoes, cucumber, celery, radishes, sweetcorn, coloured peppers and black olives, all diced up to a uniform size. Try to have even quantities of each.

A can of chickpeas (you can use any smaller pulses, but drain them and rinse them well).
Sweetcorn (frozen or tinned), drained.
Chopped coriander leaves.
Harissa paste.
Olive oil.
Lime juice.

Once the carbs are cooked, you can assemble the dish. You can cool the pasta or grains, but this is actually rather nice served warm.

Tip all the chopped vegetables on top of the carbs in a large bowl. Tip in a tablespoon of harissa paste (rose harissa is even nicer), two tablespoons of lime juice, and a good splash or two of olive oil, then most of the coriander leaves, and mix it all well. It should look like an edible rainbow!

Serve with the rest of the coriander leaves scattered on top, and maybe a dollop of plain yoghurt or plain dairy-alternative yoghurt.

## CERES'S CARROT CAKE

*This is a recipe I have used for many years, and it has certainly come in very handy for coven birthdays and other celebrations because it can easily be tweaked to create a vegan-friendly cake. My high priest, the smug madam, can make perfect vegan chocolate cakes, which rise, fluffy and sexy, with no eggs in the mix and do not collapse when they come out of the oven. I have never been able to achieve this!*

*However, any cake recipe which uses vegetables will work without eggs. I have seen recipes for courgettes used in place of carrots and raw beetroot (not the kind pickled in vinegar!) used in chocolate cake. These do not sound very appetising, yet they do produce very successful cakes without eggs, and in the case of the beetroot, it gives a wonderful earthy flavour and 'red velvet' colouring to the cake. Bananas also work rather well, but carrot cake is a guaranteed favourite which even the fussiest eaters will enjoy. It's quite flexible, and you can make a layer cake, a traybake or cupcakes.*

### *You will need:*

280g plain white flour.
2 teaspoons of baking soda.

1 teaspoon salt.
1½ teaspoons of ground cinnamon.
Tiny pinch of allspice or clove.
250g margarine.
200g granulated sugar.
200g dark brown sugar.
1 teaspoon of vanilla extract.
4 large eggs (omit if you have vegans at the meal).
300g carrots, peeled and grated.
50g chopped pecans or walnuts.
50g raisins.
Frosting.

**METHOD:** Heat the oven to 175°C, gas mark 4, and grease and line the tins you are using – this amount will fill 2 eight-inch tins.

First, melt the margarine gently over a low heat and set aside to cool slightly. If you are making a vegan version of this cake, make sure you use vegan margarine, which is now readily available in supermarkets, and omit the eggs.

Mix the flour, salt, baking powder, and the spices together in a bowl.

Using a wooden spoon or an electric hand whisk, beat the melted margarine with the two kinds of sugar and the vanilla extract in a large bowl. If you are using eggs, beat them in as well.

Now sift the flour mixture into the margarine mixture and fold in with a metal spoon or a rubber spatula, making sure there are no pockets of dry flour.

Now mix in the grated carrots, and when you have a nice well-mixed batter, stir in the dried fruit and the nuts.

Turn the cake batter into the prepared cake tins and bake until the tops of the cake layers are springy when touched and when a skewer inserted into the centre of the cake comes out clean, around 35 to 45 mins.

Cool the cakes in the pans for 15 mins, then turn out onto the cooling racks, peel off the parchment paper and cool completely. *Hack: if using the vegan version of the recipe, pop the cakes into the freezer for a few hours. Without eggs, they are very fragile, and icing them is a nightmare. Freezing them stabilises them so you can work without them shattering.

I have never had any luck with the traditional frosting for carrot cake, which is made from cream cheese, but I find a nice buttercream works just as well – you need about 200g icing sugar and 100g margarine, and I like to add a little pink food colouring because it looks pretty with the cake. Sandwich the two cake halves together with half the frosting and spread the rest on top; decorate with walnuts or sugar sprinkles.

## DESCENT

**The Autumn Equinox, usually around 21st September.** The sun enters Libra some time between 19th and 23rd September and paves the way for the autumn and the ensuing winter. This Sabbat, when again night equals day in length, has previously been called Mabon, but many pagans are moving away from this nomenclature, which was arbitrarily assigned to the festival in the 1970s by the US occultist Aidan Kelly and is not relevant to this time of year, being the name of a Welsh God who appears in the King Arthur stories. My own community has settled on 'Descent' as a more appropriate name for this time, in reference to the descent of the Goddess into the Underworld to seek Her Lord. Historically, pagan belief in all parts of the world is full of stories that sought to explain the disappearance of the sun and the flowers as winter set in, and a Goddess mourning for or following her lover or her child into the Underworld is a popular theme.

### *Descent Fare*

Apples are associated with several of the festivals, but at Descent they really come into their own, as most of them are either ripe and fruiting right now or have been gathered and stored, and as cider they certainly play a large role in the festival. Other fruits too are important; the late plums and pears of the country garden and the nuts gathered in the hedgerow all play a part in this second harvest.

Foods like roasted chicken, herb-infused dishes, and apple cider are used to celebrate the harvest and honour the bounty of the earth, as are pomegranates … associated with the story of the abduction of Persephone by Hades. If foraging is your thing, look now for wild mushrooms (never eat these without lots of research and checking that they are not poisonous!) and hazelnuts, our most common wild nut. Or you can just buy these at all times of year in the shops. And you can grow your own mushrooms using a kit: these will give you a lovely glut of mushrooms every few days (they freeze well, once cooked).

Another fruit strongly associated with Descent is the humble blackberry, which you can find growing abundantly and free to pick in any hedgerow. Anyone can gather them, as they are easily recognised and do not resemble any poisonous fruit that grows in the UK. The glistening, jewel-like berries are sweet and perfect for pies and crumbles, but can also be used in the recipe below, for easy finger food.

### AUTUMN NUT AND MUSHROOM PASTA

*This creamy and sumptuous dish is suitable for vegetarians and can be adapted for vegans as suggested in the ingredients. The hazelnuts should be blanched and roughly chopped, then toasted, but of course you can buy them already done. I would choose a rustic type of mushroom for this, such as chestnut mushrooms or one of those mixed punnets supermarkets sometimes have, for their lovely colour.*

*You will need:*

250g mushrooms.
50g hazelnuts, chopped and toasted.
1 tablespoon of vegan margarine.
1 tablespoon of olive oil.
2–3 garlic cloves, peeled and chopped.
1 tablespoon of onion powder (optional: I love this versatile ingredient, but not everyone has it in their cupboard).
250g pasta: any kind you like, but small shapes work better in this dish.
200ml crème fraiche, or a vegan dairy alternative.
Zest and juice of a lemon.
Handful of fresh parsley, finely chopped.
100g Parmesan cheese, grated – you can get vegan Parmesan now.
Salt and pepper.

**METHOD:** Pick over the mushrooms and chop them into bite-sized pieces. Heat the oil and margarine together gently in a pan and add the garlic and mushrooms, frying them gently until softened and tender. Meanwhile, bring a pan of salted water to the boil and cook the pasta until just tender.

When the mushrooms are cooked, add the lemon juice, crème fraiche, onion powder (if using) and season to taste. Stir in about 80g of the Parmesan and add the parsley at the last moment: you don't want it cooked and limp.

Drain the pasta and add to the sauce, mixing it all well. Turn into a serving dish and sprinkle over the last 20g of cheese. This will keep warm in a very slow oven or hostess trolley while your ritual takes place or can be taken out for outdoor events, as it is quite nice served cold.

### FREYJA'S FRUITY CRUMBLE SQUARES

*These are a handy standby when you need to take some food to share at a ritual, because they are quick to prepare from stuff you will mostly have in your cupboard, as well as easy to handle outside without plates. This amount will make about 12 little square portions. Changing the butter for vegan margarine and using water instead of milk makes these suitable for everyone.*

*You will need:*

**For the base** –
200g plain flour.
70g granulated sugar.
¼ teaspoon salt.
140g butter, chilled and cut into small pieces.
Small amount of milk.

**Filling** -
500g blackberries, hulled and washed but raw (you can even use them straight from the freezer), OR 500g chopped raw apples (add ½ teaspoon of ground cinnamon), OR you can even use a jar of jam, preferably homemade.

**For the crumble topping** -
200g plain flour.
100g light brown sugar.
100g granulated sugar.
½ teaspoon salt.
½ teaspoon of baking powder.
½ teaspoon of ground cinnamon.
150g rolled oats.
150g butter, chilled and cut into small pieces.
A little milk.
Icing sugar for dusting (optional).

**METHOD:** Preheat your oven to 190°C, gas mark 5, with the oven shelf in the middle of the oven. Line a rectangular medium baking pan with non-stick paper with some overhang on the sides. Lightly spritz the paper with cooking spray.

**Make the base** – In a large bowl, rub together the base ingredients: flour, sugar, butter, and salt until the mixture appears sandy and forms fine crumbs. Add the almond extract and the milk carefully and combine until a dough is formed. Press into the prepared tin in an even layer. Bake until the centre is just set and the edges are just beginning to turn light brown, around 20 mins. Remove from the oven, leaving it on, and assemble the squares.

**Make the oat crumble topping** – While the base is baking, mix the flour, salt, baking powder, sugar, and oats in a bowl.

Rub the butter into the flour, sugar, oats, and salt mixture until crumbly. Add a little milk to pull together.
**Assemble the squares –** Spread the fruit over the hot crust layer. Spread crumble topping in an even layer over the fruit and press down well.

Return it to the oven and bake for 25–30 minutes, until the crumble topping is light golden brown. Let it stand at room temperature in the baking pan until completely cooled.

Dust with icing sugar – or crunchy demerara – and slice into squares.

### PERSEPHONE'S POMEGRANATE PUNCH

*Pomegranates are associated with the descent of the Goddess because of their role in the forced marriage of Persephone, who was dragged off into Hades by the Lord of the Dead himself, without so much as an engagement ring. Because she ate some pomegranate seeds, in this Greek legend she was not allowed to return home to mum. As I have noted, pomegranates do not have much flavour, but as a syrup (grenadine), they add a sweet kick and a pretty colour to any drink.*

*You will need:*

500ml apple juice.
500ml pineapple juice.
500ml cider (omit if you want an alcohol-free punch).
100ml grenadine.
½ teaspoon of ground cinnamon, or stir cinnamon sticks into the bowl.
Mint leaves and orange slices to decorate.
Crushed ice.

**METHOD:** Simply mix all the liquid ingredients together and pour into a bowl or large jug over the ice. You can add sugar syrup (boil together 100g sugar and 100ml water) if you prefer a very sweet punch. Garnish and serve to 'oohs' from your pagan friends.

## ESBAT

The one thing I make every month is the mooncakes which we use for the *Cakes and Wine* part of the ritual at the end, before we open the circle. These need to be suitable for everyone, so I have to be careful not to add any milk or use butter but to stick to margarine that is 100% plant-based. Fortunately this is readily available in the shops nowadays. Of course, you may have additional requirements, such as a covener who is gluten-intolerant, which is a game-changer. My own preference would be to provide an alternative, such as a bought gluten-free snack, and place on the main plate but carefully separated from the ordinary ones with a buffer of tinfoil, as even a crumb containing wheat flour can make a gluten-intolerant person quite unwell.

### MOONCAKES – MY RECIPE

*This could not be simpler, and I usually make a large quantity of the dough and keep it in the freezer ready to thaw and make more cakes when needed.*

*You will need:*

100g plain flour.
50g vegan margarine.
30g caster sugar.

Ground spices: these are chosen for their magical properties, such as prosperity, protection, wellbeing, etc., and a pinch only added, as some are quite strong.
Pinch of salt (this also has a magical significance, as well as improving the flavour).

**METHOD:** Preheat the oven to 180°C and grease or line a flat baking sheet.

Sift the flour into a bowl with the sugar, salt, and spices, and rub the fat in until you have that breadcrumby texture. Add a little cold water, barely enough to draw it all together into a dough, and chill in the fridge for 30 minutes or so. Then roll out to about 3mm thickness and create your mooncakes with a plain (not fluted) round cutter. Just attack the dough from the edge and then make another cut further in, to make a crescent shape.

Place the crescents on the baking sheet and bake for around 10 minutes – watch them, as they cook very quickly. You can also freeze cooked cakes, but they are nicer when eaten freshly baked. For special occasions – or just because Esbats are about magic – why not sprinkle them with cake glitter?

And here below is another recipe from Lady Willow (one of our coven elders), which is even nicer. These are buttery and crumbly – and vegan.

### MOON BISCUITS

*You will need:*

120g margarine.
60g golden caster sugar.

60g plain flour
130g rolled oats.
½ teaspoon salt.
Pinch of baking powder.

**METHOD:** Cream together the margarine and sugar. Once blended, slowly mix in the other ingredients. Then place the blended ingredients onto a floured surface. Pat out with your hands until the mixture is as flat as possible. Do not use a rolling pin, as the mixture is too soft and it will stick. Cut out using a moon crescent-shaped cutter. If you don't have a moon-crescent cutter, it is possible to make this shape by overlapping a circular cutter.

Place on greaseproof paper and bake at 180°C until golden brown, about 18 minutes. Then place on a rack to cool.

These are a good range of recipes to get you started or provide an idea when you want one for a Sabbat, but how about when you are planning a ritual dedicated to one of the pagan Gods or Goddesses? My own coven frequently holds rituals dedicated to one of our favourite deities, or perhaps to introduce coveners to a lesser-known deity, and of course food will play an important part in this – and not just food to offer to the Gods, but to fill the tums of your worshippers. In the next chapter, we will look at food for such rituals.

CHAPTER NINE

# Dedicated Dishes

"Dost thou think, because thou art virtuous, there shall be no more cakes and ale?"

– Shakespeare: *Twelfth Night*.

The world of pagan cooking goes on into further territories, of course: how about when you hold a ritual dedicated to a particular deity and wish to carry these correspondences through into the meal after the ritual? Magical groups often share a meal after the ritual, as we have seen, and in some cases *during* the ritual, as part of an immersive spiritual experience. In tables of *correspondences* for any God or Goddess, you will find foods that are considered appropriate for Him or Her, and recipes – or whole menus – can easily be created around these divine gustatory preferences. But sometimes only modern foods will do, or maybe the historically appropriate foods may not be available. Do not despair: just because we are pagans does not mean we have to stick to the foods our Bronze Age or classical period forebears would have eaten: God and Goddess are with us *now*, and They know all about the Internet and AI and cloud computing and cryptocurrency ... and FOOD!

There are thousands upon thousands of pagan Gods: Ancient Egypt alone honoured over 3,000 different deities, from the state God Amen-Ra to local Gods honoured only by the peasants of certain localities and their families, or the stone carvers associated with a burial area. The Romans, with their own large pantheon and countless smaller Gods, and their habit of adopting any foreign deity that crossed their path, were not far behind. Creating a recipe book to please every deity on the planet would be the work of a lifetime, so I will just give a few examples of what you can do with a little information and a little imagination. In each case, the food must be prepared mindfully, using the best ingredients available, or that you can afford, and also eaten mindfully, with prayers and libation. A place should be laid for the God or Goddess being honoured, and food placed on His or Her plate: treat this divine visitor as the most honoured guest. The general correspondences of the deity should also be taken into consideration: the colours of the dishes and cloth, the flowers on the table, and any symbols perhaps used to decorate the food.

## ARTEMIS

This moon Goddess is the twin sister of the sun God Apollo and has a wealth of legends about Her. The Ancients saw a bow in the shape of the new moon and associated this with this virgin Goddess, who is also a Goddess of the hunt. She was so closely associated with deer that this animal is sacred to Her, and on occasions She has taken the form of a doe or turned others into deer if they have displeased Her. Venison and goat meat were traditionally eaten at Her festivals, so unless you are preparing a meal for vegetarians and vegans, a nice venison casserole would be an appropriate dish for an Artemis feast.

One way around the meat problem is to offer deer at the meal – but make them from cake or biscuit. At a spring festival, Artemis was offered cakes made from flour, honey and sesame seeds, baked in the shape of stags. I am sorry to say that at some of Her festivals, live animals, game, wild creatures and birds were thrown into a fire as sacrifices to Her. Another offering that was made to Her was round mooncakes, and these are very appropriate and can be made to look beautiful as well.

## MOON GODDESS CAKES

*White cake is made without egg yolks or butter to give a very light, fluffy, crumbly texture that feels more like a meringue or macaroon than a cake. Because it can also be very dry, it is a good idea to add some colourless vegetable oil to it, as in this recipe.*

*You will need:*

120g plain flour, well sifted.
4 eggs, whites only.
90g caster sugar.
2 tablespoons of flavourless vegetable oil.
A pinch of salt.
A pinch of baking powder.
Vanilla extract, or almond is also good.

**METHOD:** Preheat the oven to 150°C, gas mark 2.

Whisk the egg whites with the pinch of salt until they are stiff, as though making a meringue. With the beaters still going, start to tip in the caster sugar, a little at a time, and continue to whisk until it is stiff and glossy. Take a metal spoon or a silicone blade and add the flour, baking powder, and flavouring, mixing gently until all is well mixed, with no pockets of dry flour.

Bake the cake in one of the ways below until done in the middle, about 35 mins for one cake, or 20–25 mins for individual ones. Or, if you have time, you can place it in a very cool oven (60–100°C) for several hours and set it exactly like a meringue.

This gives a pure white cake, though it will have a golden crust if you have the oven a little too high. The cake mix can be treated in several ways. You can ice the cake as it is, and decorate it with silver dragees or stars or edible silver glitter. You can tip the cake onto a board and cut it with round cutters to give many little full moons, and then decorate these individually. You can spoon the mixture into cupcake cases, bake and then ice and decorate, or even dollop spoonfuls of the mixture onto a lined baking sheet and shape them into round mounds with a spatula or by using a greased round pastry cutter as a mould, before levelling the top and baking as before. And if you are any good at piping icing, you can add a crescent moon or a magical sigil to the top as well.

## BAST

One of the best known of the animal Gods of Egypt, Bast's likeness can be seen in all sorts of places: temples, wall paintings, and statuettes. The cat was a deeply sacred animal in Ancient Egypt (and continues to be pretty popular today!). Bast is a party girl, a Goddess of love, sex, beauty, and pleasure, and She is connected to the cow Goddess Hat-Hor, who is also a Goddess of love and beauty, and to the lioness Goddess Sekhmet, who is nothing of the sort but a fierce warrior and destroyer of evil.

Feasts at rituals dedicated to Bast can include all sorts of pleasure foods, including chocolate (which the Egyptians would not have known, of course), sweet cakes, and honey and wine (which they did). Actually, She is associated with a notorious Festival of Drunkenness, which was held regularly in Egypt and was a sort of rowdy, colourful carnival involving music and parades, costumes, a great deal of beer and wine, and no doubt some scandalous behaviour.

The festival seems to have been a celebration of the best-known story associated with Sekhmet, Bast's scarier alter ego (in some versions with Hat-Hor, or as Hat-Hor taking Sekhmet's shape). The Great Lioness was sent to punish sinful mankind by Ra, king of the Gods – in much the same way as the biblical Yahweh sent the Flood – and She set about killing people at an appalling rate. Alarmed that His people would be completely wiped out, when He only intended a warning, Ra tried to recall Her. But She was intoxicated by the taste of blood, and would not listen. Ra had an idea. He mixed red ochre, a naturally occurring red clay, with a large amount of beer and poured it into a valley for Sekhmet to find. She thought it was blood and started to drink greedily, eventually becoming quite drunk and falling asleep, thus leaving the rest of humanity alone.

A drunken coven is not a nice sight, I imagine, and obviously people have to drive to get home. But wine and beer can be used judiciously as part of a ritual to Bast or Sekhmet, or Their names can be invoked at a proper celebration party, and toasts made to Them in champagne. You could also use wine and beer in the cooking, so that sherry trifle and a wine-infused casserole or a salad dressed with good-quality wine vinegar would also be suitable for the supper after a ritual to Bast. As She is a cat, a fish supper would also be an appropriate post-ritual meal for the coven, but my own preference would be for something that I had made myself, magically and mindfully, with Her name on my lips as I mixed the ingredients. So I have married the flavour of alcohol with chocolate in honour of Her pleasure Goddess attributes, and I give here a recipe from a sister priestess. I am afraid this is not one for vegans, or for anyone who has issues around alcohol. If this is a problem for anyone in your group, you will need an alternative dessert recipe for those members.

### LADY WILLOW'S RUM BROWNIES

*You will need:*

350g plain chocolate.
175g butter.
3 eggs.
3 tablespoons of dark rum.
1 tablespoon of rum flavouring.
100g self-raising flour.
1 tablespoon of cocoa powder (not drinking chocolate!).
225g golden caster sugar.

**METHOD:** Grease and line an 11-inch by 8-inch tin. Preheat oven to 180°C, gas mark 5.

Melt the chocolate and the butter in a bowl over a saucepan of hot water.

Beat the eggs with the caster sugar, rum, and flavouring in a bowl and gradually sift in the flour and cocoa powder until all are combined. When the chocolate and butter have melted, add this to the egg mixture and beat together well.

Pour into the prepared tin and bake in the oven for 30 minutes. Cool completely before cutting into portions.

## DEMETER

This Greek grain Goddess, whose Latin name 'Ceres' gives us our word 'cereal', is one of the main protagonists in the legend of the abduction of Persephone by Hades, which was also the subject of the famous Eleusinian mysteries. No one now knows exactly how these mysteries were enacted, but some substances were certainly consumed at them which I would not recommend, including hallucinogens based on the poisonous fungus *Amanita muscaria* (the fly agaric) and the drink kykeon, which was made from barley, honey and pennyroyal. Pennyroyal can have unwanted effects, especially on pregnant women, so if you want to recreate this drink, use common mint instead.

Demeter was above all the Goddess of harvest and grain, so you can't really go wrong with fresh-baked bread, especially sprinkled with poppy seeds, as the corn poppy was also one of Her symbols. But another lovely way to honour Her is to rediscover a rather old-fashioned dish called 'frumenty', which our ancestors would have enjoyed for special occasions, especially Christmas, but it is also wonderful for a special breakfast or supper and deserves to be resurrected. It is suitable for vegans.

### FULGENT FRUMENTY

Take 200g of cracked wheat or pearl barley, or you can use porridge oats, which do not need the lengthy cooking in this recipe.

Measure the grains in a jug, then add an equal measure of milk and another of water or just all water for vegans.

Pour the mixture into a pan and add whatever spices you like, starting with a good teaspoon of saffron strands. This is expensive but gives such a wonderful golden colour and fragrance to the dish for a special occasion. You can add any other spices you like: cinnamon is obviously a good choice, or ginger or ground nutmeg or cardamom would work well. Add a pinch of salt.

Cook very slowly for two or three hours until thickened and tender – this can be done much more easily in a slow cooker. Now add 100g of raisins or sultanas, 2–3 tablespoons of chopped nuts and the zest and juice of an orange. Reheat as necessary and top with a good dollop of cream (plant-based for vegans). Fit for a goddess!

## DIONYSUS

This is the name of a fertility God from Ancient Greece who is also inextricably associated with wine and drunkenness – His other name is Bacchus, as in 'Bacchanalian'. Again, the 21st-century problem is that of our modern drink-driving laws, but Dionysus can be honoured with the raw material for wine: grapes. And as He is a vegetation God, He can also be honoured with all sorts of vegetables, especially those grown and used in Greece. Dolmades, a Greek dish of herbs and rice wrapped in vine leaves (which Dionysus wears on His head in many portrayals), would be especially appropriate for a ritual feast for this God. You can buy the leaves tinned in larger supermarkets or online, or you may have a kind friend with a grapevine! Here is a simple recipe:

### DIONYSUS'S DOLMADES

*You will need:*

Vine leaves.
100g long-grain rice, cooked until tender.
1 heaped tablespoon of chopped herbs: I suggest tarragon, basil, and thyme.
The juice and grated zest of a lemon.
2–3 garlic cloves, crushed and chopped.
Olive oil.
Pepper and salt.

**METHOD:** First deal with the leaves. If they are fresh from a vine, you will need to cook them in boiling water until they are limp, but not falling apart. Then plunge them in cold water. If they are tinned, it is still a good idea to blanch them like this to make them tender.

Now chop the herbs and garlic and mix with the cooked rice and also the lemon zest. Season it well, and add a good glug of oil and lemon juice to moisten the mix.

Lay out the leaves, with their shiny side down and veiny side (the underside of the leaf) uppermost, pile some of the filling in the centre, and fold the leaf up into a little parcel: you may need to use more than one if they are small. This might take a little practice, but if you are used to stuffing pancakes or tortillas, it will be easy.

Lay all the dolmades into a baking dish that has been well-oiled, and sprinkle with more lemon juice. Bake in a hot oven for about 20 minutes, really just to reheat. Dolmades can also contain meat, typically minced lamb, but this vegan recipe will be suitable for all.

## EPONA

This Romano-Celtic horse Goddess is a Goddess of the Underworld, but is also associated with fertility and fruitfulness, and She is sometimes depicted carrying sheaves of corn and baskets of fruit. She may be the inspiration behind the famous white horses carved into the chalk hills of southern England, and Her name gives us our English word 'pony'. Some scholars believe She is the inspiration for the traditional Mari Llywd 'hobby-horses', formed from a horse's skull and draperies, which you will often see at fairs and Neopagan events.

I feel She might be better honoured in the wide open spaces, rather than in someone's dining room, and a picnic would be a great way to worship Her with food. The Celts ate a lot of grains and also much foraged food, wild fruit, such as blackberries, sloes, wild strawberries, and bullace, as well as nuts and honey. Here is a simple but healthy and delicious dessert salad based on pearl barley. If you omit the honey and substitute golden syrup, then it will be suitable for vegans. It travels well but does need spoons.

### EPONA'S WILD SALAD

*You will need:*

200g pearl barley.
100g hazelnuts, coarsely chopped and toasted.

3 tablespoons of runny honey.
Fruit: try to choose fruit which is native to the UK, even if you cannot find wild fruit. Strawberries, raspberries, blackberries, plums, and even chopped apples will work well.
A little ground spice, maybe cinnamon or ginger, will give a little extra flavour.

**METHOD:** Cook the pearl barley in boiling water until tender, about 25 minutes, then drain, rinse and leave to cool.

Chop the apples, leaving the skin on unless it is very tough, and place in acidulated water (water with lemon juice added). Chop the fruit, leaving smaller berries like raspberries whole. When you are ready to make the salad, drain the apples and mix the nuts and all the fruit in with the cooked barley. Drizzle the honey over the salad and mix in well with any spices you are using, saving a little bit to drizzle over the top for a nice shine.

## GANESH

This Hindu God, with His elephant's head, must be familiar to most people, as He is so popular with Hindus throughout India and in the West. But He is also very popular with Western Neopagans, who cherish Him for His attribute as Remover of Obstacles. The son of the God Shiva, Ganesh lost His head and was given an elephant's in its place – for which there are many different stories in explanation. His head and His somewhat portly frame give Him a jolly look, and stories describe Him as a lover of good things, especially sweets. Often depicted with many arms, He is also commonly shown holding a sweetmeat in one hand, and He is also a God of books, learning, and intelligence.

Ganesh's favourites are two kinds of sweets traditionally offered to Him at festivals: laddu, which are little syrupy balls with peanuts and sesame seeds, and modak, coconut- and sugar-filled wheat or rice pastries. Because He is also associated with the base chakra, it is traditional to offer Him red sweets, and these would be best served on a red dish.

How about these as an offering to Ganesh when He has removed an obstacle for you?

## ELEPHANT BALLS

*These are made in seconds in a food processor, and if you serve them at a ritual, the plate will be empty just as quickly.*

*You will need:*

100g white chocolate.
About 1 tablespoon of golden syrup.
100g stoned dates.
100g raisins or sultanas.
50g glacé cherries, chopped.
6 tablespoons of rice flour or even fine porridge oats.
Desiccated coconut or sesame seeds.

**METHOD:** Place the chocolate in a bowl over a pan of hot water until it is quite softened but *not melted*. Turn it into the food processor goblet and add the flour and dates, and blitz for a moment until the dates are chopped. Now add the rest of the ingredients, apart from the syrup and the coconut/sesame seeds. Mix again, but not for too long, as you don't want to liquidise the fruit. Now drizzle in the syrup, very slowly, until the mixture starts to come together – you may not need it all.

Take the mixture out of the processor and form it into small balls on a board, using wet hands. Do not flour the board, as these balls will not be cooked and raw wheat flour is not very nice. Roll the balls in desiccated coconut or sesame seeds to coat, and chill in the fridge (they also freeze well).

If you wanted to make these even more appropriate for this deity, you could use red 'chocolate' in place of the white to give a red sweetmeat. Many stores and shopping malls sell 'pick 'n' mix' loose sweets, and it is possible to find red chocolate-style candy buttons, or you can buy them online. They behave just like chocolate.

## HECATE

This Goddess, so dear to modern witches, was honoured in Ancient Greece with the Deipnon, a series of sacrifices held at the dark moon and involving not only offerings of food, flowers and incense but general domestic practice like cleaning – making a clean sweep before the new month began. The Deipnon was comprised of a sacrifice for guilt and reparation, especially to the dead who may have been insulted or injured in some way; another for purification of the household; and a sacred supper which was laid out at crossroads – sacred to Her – and no doubt usually consumed by the poor. My own preference month-to-month is to donate to the local food bank, blessing the items in Her name before I deliver them to the depot (my local one is run by a church group – if only they knew!). I generally try to include dog food in the donation, as dogs, especially black ones, are sacred to Hecate, and I have got my WI as well as my coven donating items.

However, a Hecate supper for the coven is also appropriate for Her festivals and at dark moons, and there is a selection of foods which are appropriate for this.

I would generally start by acknowledging Her origins in Ancient Greece and include items like wine, olives, and even some Greek specialities like feta cheese on the table or even spanakopita (see recipe in Chapter Eight under Ostara dishes). A number of foods are favoured by this Goddess, particularly strong-smelling vegetables like onions, leeks and garlic, honey and red mullet. In Ancient Greece, Her followers would have eaten dog as part of Her rituals (and a dog might have been sacrificed as a sort of scapegoat during one of the rituals), but modern witches would probably draw the line at that! (However, there's nothing to stop you doing this symbolically, by having a dog made from chocolate cake or shortbread.) So, a Hecate supper might centre on a fish dish, surrounded by new-baked bread, wine (how about some Greek retsina?), olives and olive oil, eggs (the ancients would have set out raw eggs, but modern witches will be too aware of the health hazards attached to eating these), vegetable dishes that include onions, leeks and garlic, perhaps a frittata to use these and the eggs, and maybe some sweet cakes made with honey.

Here is a simple vegetarian pizza recipe that uses some of the foods sacred to Hecate. What, pizza? I hear you ask … are we getting our cultures mixed up? My reply to that is that Hecate is worshipped in Naples, as well as in Athens, London, Paris, New York, and doubtless in a thousand other places that know not Greek cuisine. Anyway, if you look at the ingredients, it is about as Greek as it is Italian.

## POLYBOTEIRA PIZZA

*Polyboteira is one of Hecate's many epithets and means 'giver of much nourishment'.*

*You will need:*

One large pizza base made with bread dough.
1 onion.
3 cloves of garlic.
1 large leek.
1 tin of tomatoes, or about 8 fresh ones, chopped.
Olive oil.
1 tablespoon each of chopped basil and chopped parsley.
200g crumbled feta cheese.

**METHOD:** Preheat the oven to 180°C, gas mark 4. Slice up the onion finely and cook gently in a little olive oil. When it is transparent but not brown, add the garlic cloves, finely chopped, and the leek, finely sliced. Cook for a few minutes until just tender. Add the tomatoes and stir in well, chopping if necessary with the spatula. Add the herbs, and season well to taste.

Lay the dough base on a well-oiled baking sheet, and place the sauce on top, spreading it out evenly almost to the edges. Top with crumbled feta cheese as liked, or omit and pour over extra olive oil instead for vegans: the pizza will still be delicious. Place in the hot oven for about 20 minutes until the dough is cooked and the cheese is melting.

## LIR AND MANANNAN

Manannan Mac Lir is a God of the sea and of the Underworld in Celtic beliefs, and there is a wealth of legends concerning Him. His father was the sea God Lir (or Llyr in Welsh), but Manannan seems to have taken over or inherited His father's position and title. He is also said to have given His name to the Isle of Man.

As these deities are sea Gods, one's thoughts naturally turn to fish and seafood, but this may not please all the attendees, and Manannan is associated with some landlubber food, such as beef and apples.

Another suggestion is a favourite Celtic dish that uses seaweed, and you can even gather it yourself for nothing if you live near the sea. Welsh laverbread can be bought online or in some larger supermarkets. It is made from a common shoreline seaweed, *Porphyra umbilicalis*, which is washed well, boiled and chopped and has quite a strong savoury flavour, which I think is delicious. The Welsh eat it on toast like Marmite, or spread it on bread or just eat it on its own. I have also had laverbread sausages, with laverbread added to the pork mixture, and seen laverbread cheese and other laverbread comestibles on sale in Welsh markets. It can also be made into little cakes, which are commonly served with bacon and eggs for breakfast in Wales. But as they are an excellent vegan product, you could also make a vegan breakfast or supper from them by adding tomatoes, mushrooms and baked beans to the plate.

### LLYR'S LAVERBREAD CAKES

*You will need:*

120g laverbread (the product tends to come in 120g packs).
100g fine rolled oats.
Plain flour.
Lemon juice.
Oil for frying.

**METHOD:** Put the laverbread into a bowl and add a tablespoon of lemon juice, which regulates the flavour and strength of the product. Or you could add Worcestershire sauce, if you prefer.

Tip in the oats and mix everything together into a sort of dough. If you find it is a little too runny, add some of the flour. Do not add salt!

Now shape the mixture into little patties, just as though you were making rissoles, on a floured board, and heat some oil in your frying pan. When it is hot but not smoking, place the patties in the pan and fry on both sides until golden and crisp.

## ODIN

Many modern pagans honour the Allfather, the polymath ruler of the Norse Gods, and would wish to honour Him at their feasts. However, a quick look at His personal diet regime will reveal that … He doesn't eat! His faithful wolves Geri and Freki sit beside Him at mealtimes, no doubt doing all the things your own pet dog does when it thinks it is missing out on a tasty treat, and Odin feeds them from His own plate, giving them all His meat and consuming only wine Himself. This is somewhat restricting for anyone planning an Odin feast, but you can still set out Norse-style food and make the wine jug the centre of the festivities (this is, of course, not suitable for anyone with issues around alcohol). This spiced wine uses some items you would find in nature in Britain but also imported spices, which you might think are not really appropriate for a God of Northern Europe and Scandinavia. However, when you look into the travels of the Norsemen, you will see they probably encountered many more foreign foods and flavourings than you might imagine.

### THE ALLFATHER'S WINE CUP

*You will need:*

A bottle of a fairly stalwart red wine, such as Rioja.
3 tablespoons of honey or (for a vegan-friendly drink) a similar quantity of sugar syrup made by boiling sugar and water.
Two good handfuls of sloes, crushed (if you can't get sloes, or it isn't the right time of year, use plums or cherries).
A cinnamon stick.
Half a dozen bay leaves.
A lemon, juiced and with the peel shaved off in strips.

**METHOD:** Heat the wine gently and stir in all the other ingredients, leaving to steep as long as possible before straining and serving. You can serve cold or reheat.

## OSIRIS

The great God who embodied the fertility of Egypt and brought the annual flooding of the Nile (this was long before the Aswan Dam put a collar and lead on this great waterway) is most strongly associated with grain and its products: bread and beer – both hugely important in Ancient Egypt. The builders of the pyramids (who were not slaves but agricultural labourers doing a sort of National Service) are known to have held the first recorded industrial action, going on strike for more bread, beer, and onions!

Osiris was believed by the Nile Valley people to have been an ancient king of Egypt who brought civilisation and agriculture to the people of the Nile Valley and taught them to abandon savage practices such as cannibalism. He was so loved that His brother Set murdered Him out of jealousy, cutting His body into 14 pieces and scattering them across the land of Egypt. However, Osiris's queen Isis found them all and put Him back together again, that He might be whole in the afterlife. Only one piece was not found: the penis, which had been eaten by a fish. Osiris is generally shown wrapped like a mummy but with His face and hands bare, and these are coloured green – not to indicate putrefaction, but because of His association with fertility and vegetation.

A dish of vegetables would certainly be an appropriate dish at an Osiris ritual, especially if it included onions, leeks and garlic, which were all loved by the Ancient Egyptians (and still are to this day). But His association with grain is even stronger – so, sorry, it's bread again, but how could it not be? Try this one: its flavour is just superb, and it goes very well with the side dish below it, which the Egyptians would have enjoyed as well. Both recipes are suitable for vegans.

## BEER BREAD AND ONIONS, TOMB BUILDERS' STYLE

*You will need:*

500g strong flour: I would suggest using a wholemeal or even a granary flour with kibbled wheat in it. Egyptian bread was not known for its softness!
100ml of oil.
About 300ml bitter or stout beer.
1 sachet easy-action yeast.
1 teaspoon of salt.

**METHOD:** Put the flour and salt into a large bowl (or you can use a breadmaker or other mixer). Glug in the oil: this may seem rather a lot, but Egyptian bread was heavily oily, rather like modern croissants. Sprinkle the yeast into the flour.

Warm the beer in a pan until it is very warm, but not too hot to put your hand in. Now start pouring it into the flour mixture, mixing as you go. Be careful not to add too much liquid: you only want enough to draw the dry ingredients together into a dough, which should not be too sloppy. Continue kneading, either by hand or in a machine, for about five minutes. The dough should smell wonderful, and, after kneading, should be silky, not sticky.

Shape it into a round loaf on a floured board and leave to rise until it is roughly doubled in size. The round shape was very traditional: in fact, the Egyptian hieroglyph *ta*, which is the letter T and can also mean 'bread' or 'cake', is just a small semicircle, which was clearly based on the shape of a loaf viewed from the side.

Heat the oven to 220°C, gas mark 7, and place the bread inside. After a few minutes, turn down the heat a little, and bake for 25–30 minutes, until golden brown.

**To serve:** Heat a little oil in a pan and gently fry 2 peeled and thinly sliced onions with 3 fat cloves of garlic, peeled and chopped, and 2 big leeks, finely sliced. When they are tender, season with salt and add more oil, scatter with a handful of sesame seeds and serve in a dish beside the bread.

## THE DUMB SUPPER

This meal, a very good example of eating together as ritual, is traditionally held at Samhain to honour the ancestors and the beloved dead who have passed into the Summerlands more recently. I would just say that inviting the spirit world into your dining room willy-nilly is a rather brave (and some would say silly) thing to do, because who or what might turn up in response to your open invitation is quite unpredictable, and you may end up with mischievous spirits or uncouth and angry ancestors from the distant past, or what I like to call 'beasties' – nasty elementals.

However, there is plenty you can do to protect against unwanted guests. For a start, you can limit your guest list to known individuals. For example, your grandparents – calling them by name – or you can put up protections around the space in which you will be dining, anything from a ring of salt to a full cast circle.

Just what you choose to prepare for the meal depends on many factors, including your own ethnicity. In Ireland, for example, you might serve a boiled ham with colcannon (a luscious dish of mashed potatoes and cabbage drenched in butter), soda bread, and barmbrack, a rich fruity cake. If you were Greek, you might serve Kolyva, a sweet fruit- and nut-filled version of frumenty (see above).

The table should be set very formally and ideally in mourning colours, with a black cloth, if you have one or can borrow one; black napkins (you can buy black paper napkins); black candles (you will be turning out the electric lights and using only the candles for illumination); and black or completely plain white plates. If communal dishes are served, they need to be in several containers along the table so that everyone can reach them without asking for them to be passed – as no one is supposed to speak, remember.

Bread should certainly be on the table, for all the reasons we have seen during the previous text of this book, with butter and vegan spreads. Because people will not be able to ask for things to be passed; the bread, perhaps as rolls rather than a single loaf, should be all along the table or on each person's side plate.

As Samhain is the traditional time for a dumb supper, game, such as pheasant, grouse and venison, are suitable for the meal if you have meat-eaters. The birds are easily roasted, just like a chicken, and the venison can be served as steaks, perhaps cooked with some wine, or in a rich casserole with onions, garlic, red wine, and cranberry or redcurrant jelly. If you don't like the idea of eating wild creatures (though pheasants do not strictly fall into this category, as they are reared for the shoots), why not provide dishes of artisan sausages instead – your local butcher or supermarket will have a good array of different flavoured sausages with caramelised onions, honey, herbs, apples, and all sorts of good things added. And of course, vegetarian and even vegan sausages are now easy to find in the shops, and some are quite delicious.

Side dishes should include some carbohydrates, as we all need this as the weather turns colder. Réchauffé potatoes are suitable for an autumn feast and can be as simple as boiled potatoes crushed and fried in butter and oil, or as a bubble-and-squeak-style dish of cooked potatoes and cabbage, or other vegetables, mixed together and fried.

Gourds are now at their best, and not just the traditional Halloween pumpkins. A look along the vegetable shelves will show you amazing colourful gourds you may not have seen before, in every colour and shape. The very small ones contain little flesh and are best kept to decorate your Samhain altar – or to make a centrepiece for your dumb supper table – but the medium and larger ones can be prepared in all sorts of ways, from making soups to filling them with savoury stuffings made from onions, herbs, mushrooms, and breadcrumbs.

Dessert may include apples and blackberries or other autumn fruit, perhaps as a pie or crumble, but not perhaps as a creamy and delicious sundae or trifle – the food should be plain and wholesome, not frivolous or showy.

Finally, with the coffee, or instead of a full dessert, it may be appropriate to serve soul cakes, which are found in many cultures in the West and with many recipes, though most include spices and fruit or candied peel.

This very simple recipe below can be put together very quickly.

## TRADITIONAL SOUL CAKES

*These delicious but simple little cakes have a long history behind them. They are a little like Welsh cakes – somewhere between a scone and a pancake.*

*You will need:*

225g self-raising flour, plus extra for rolling out.
100g butter or margarine.
50g caster sugar, plus some for garnish.
75g dried currants or raisins or sultanas.
1 egg, beaten.
½ teaspoon of mixed spice.
Salt.
A little milk.

**METHOD:** Sift the flour into a bowl and add a pinch of salt. Cut up the butter or margarine into cubes and add to the flour, rubbing in between your fingertips until a breadcrumb texture is achieved. Now add the fruit, the spice, and the sugar, mixing well.

Make a well in the centre of the dry ingredients and add your egg, then mix well until a nice soft dough is achieved, adding a little milk if the mix looks too dry or fails to come together fully. Form into a dough and roll out on a floured board to about half a centimetre thick, and cut rounds from it using a plain cutter until it is all used up.

Heat a large frying pan on the stove and grease it with a little flavourless oil or melted butter or margarine. Lay as many of the cakes in as will fit and fry for about three minutes. Turn them over (they should be nice and golden on the cooked side) and repeat with the other side. Now transfer them to a cooling rack and sprinkle them with sugar while they are hot so that it sticks. If you want to be really traditional, you can make a cross on the tops with currants – or a pentagram!

The dumb supper is also associated with deities of the Underworld, and it is appropriate to honour them and make libations to them during the meal.

I hope you have enjoyed this stroll through my magical kitchen and that it has inspired you to look at your pantry door in a different way. There is a lot of magic in there … as there is a lot of magic everywhere, if you know how to look. Happy cooking!

www.ingramcontent.com/pod-product-compliance
Lightning Source LLC
LaVergne TN
LVHW010058110826
845155LV00028B/400

* 9 7 8 1 9 1 5 5 8 0 3 6 8 *